Behold

A STUDY OF THE NEW TESTAMENT

Volume 4 • Philemon–Revelation

This study belongs to:

_____

_____

THE DAILY GRACE CO.®

Behold | A Study of the New Testament, Volume 4
Copyright © 2023 by The Daily Grace Co.®
Spring, Texas. All rights reserved.

Unless otherwise noted, all Scripture quotations are taken from the Christian Standard Bible®, Copyright © 2020 by Holman Bible Publishers. Used by permission. Christian Standard Bible® and CSB® are federally registered trademarks of Holman Bible Publishers.

The extra on page 220 is adapted from *The Theology Handbook*. Copyright © 2021 by The Daily Grace Co.® Find more information about *The Theology Handbook* on page 227.

The Daily Grace Co.® exists to equip disciples to know and love God and His Word by creating beautiful, theologically rich, and accessible resources so that God may be glorified and the gospel made known.

Designed in the United States of America and printed in China.

Unlock Your Digital Study

*Did you know you can access your new study right from your phone?
Follow these simple steps, and you will be on your way to diving deeper into God's Word.*

Download The Daily Grace Co.® App
AVAILABLE FOR FREE IN THE APP STORE AND GOOGLE PLAY

Search for Your New Study
LOCATE YOUR STUDY IN THE DAILY GRACE CO.® APP

- Select the "Studies" tab found at the bottom of the home page in the app.
- Select the pink "+" button to bring up all available studies.
- Click on your new study.

Apply Your Access Code
EMAILED TO YOU AFTER PURCHASE

- Copy the access code from your email, and enter it into the "Unlock Study with Access Code" box found on our app.
- You are all set! Now that you have downloaded the app, found your study, and applied your access code, you can begin your study virtually!
- If you did not receive an email with an access code after the purchase of your new study, check your spam folder. If you still cannot find your access code, contact our Customer Delight team at info@thedailygraceco.com.

OTHER APP FEATURES

 VIDEOS COMMUNITY BIBLE BLOG PODCAST AND MORE!

Table of Contents

Introduction

Unlock Your Digital Study	3
Study Suggestions	6
How to Study the Bible	8
The Attributes of God	10
Timeline of Scripture	12
Metanarrative of Scripture	14

Week Forty-One

End-of-Week Reflection	24
Week Forty-One Application	26

Week Forty-Two

Scripture Memory	29
Day One	30
End-of-Week Reflection	40
Week Forty-Two Application	42

Week Forty-Three

Scripture Memory	45
Day One	46
End-of-Week Reflection	56
Week Forty-Three Application	58

Week Forty-Four

Scripture Memory	61
Day One	62
End-of-Week Reflection	74
Week Forty-Four Application	76

Week Forty-Five

Scripture Memory	79
Day One	80
End-of-Week Reflection	92
Week Forty-Five Application	94

Week Forty-Six

Scripture Memory	97
Day One	98
End-of-Week Reflection	110
Week Forty-Six Application	112

Week Forty-Seven

Scripture Memory	117
Day One	118
End-of-Week Reflection	128
Week Forty-Seven Application	130

Week Forty-Eight

Scripture Memory	135
Day One	136
End-of-Week Reflection	152
Week Forty-Eight Application	154

Week Forty-Nine

Scripture Memory	157
Day One	158
End-of-Week Reflection	168
Week Forty-Nine Application	170

Week Fifty

Scripture Memory	173
Day One	174
End-of-Week Reflection	184
Week Fifty Application	186

Week Fifty-One

Scripture Memory	189
Day One	190
End-of-Week Reflection	200
Week Fifty-One Application	202

Week Fifty-Two

Scripture Memory	205
Day One	206
End-of-Week Reflection	216
Week Fifty-Two Application	218

Extras

Four Millennial Views	220
What is the Gospel?	224

Editor's Note: This is the fourth of four volumes in the Behold | A Study of the New Testament *set. For this reason, this study starts with Philemon, which should technically be the fourth day of that week's content for those reading through the four-volume set sequentially. All four volumes are available for purchase at www.thedailygraceco.com.*

Study Suggestions

We believe that the Bible is true, trustworthy, and timeless and that it is vitally important for all believers. These study suggestions are intended to help you more effectively study Scripture as you seek to know and love God through His Word.

SUGGESTED STUDY TOOLS

- ☐ Bible

- ☐ Double-spaced, printed copy of the Scripture passages that this study covers (You can use a website like www.biblegateway.com to copy the text of a passage and print out a double-spaced copy to be able to mark on easily.)

- ☐ Journal to write notes or prayers

- ☐ Pens, colored pencils, and highlighters

- ☐ Dictionary to look up unfamiliar words

HOW TO USE THIS STUDY

 ### Pray

Begin your study time in prayer. Ask God to reveal Himself to you, help you understand what you are reading, and transform you with His Word (Psalm 119:18).

 ### Read Scripture

Before you read what is written in each day of the study itself, read the assigned passages of Scripture for that day. Use your double-spaced copy to circle, underline, highlight, draw arrows, and mark in any way you would like to help you dig deeper as you work through a passage.

 ### Memorize Scripture

Each week of the study begins with a memory verse. You may want to write the verse down and put it in a place where you will see it often. We also recommend spending a few minutes memorizing the verse before you complete each day's study material.

 ### Read Study Content

Read the daily written content provided for the current study day.

 ### Respond

Answer the questions that appear at the end of each study day.

How to Study the Bible

The inductive method provides tools for deeper and more intentional Bible study. To study the Bible inductively, work through the steps below after reading background information on the book.

Observation & Comprehension
KEY QUESTION: WHAT DOES THE TEXT SAY?

After reading the daily Scripture in its entirety at least once, begin working with smaller portions of the Scripture. Read a passage of Scripture repetitively, and then mark the following items in the text:

- Key or repeated words and ideas
- Key themes
- Transition words (e.g., therefore, but, because, if/then, likewise, etc.)
- Lists
- Comparisons and contrasts
- Commands
- Unfamiliar words (look these up in a dictionary)
- Questions you have about the text

Interpretation
KEY QUESTION: WHAT DOES THE TEXT MEAN?

Once you have annotated the text, work through the following steps to help you interpret its meaning:

- Read the passage in other versions for a better understanding of the text.
- Read cross-references to help interpret Scripture with Scripture.
- Paraphrase or summarize the passage to check for understanding.
- Identify how the text reflects the metanarrative of Scripture, which is the story of creation, fall, redemption, and restoration.
- Read trustworthy commentaries if you need further insight into the meaning of the passage.

Application

KEY QUESTION: HOW SHOULD THE TRUTH OF THIS PASSAGE CHANGE ME?

Bible study is not merely an intellectual pursuit. The truths about God, ourselves, and the gospel that we discover in Scripture should produce transformation in our hearts and lives. Answer the following questions and prompts as you consider what you have learned in your study:

- What attributes of God's character are revealed in the passage?
- Consider places where the text directly states the character of God, as well as how His character is revealed through His words and actions.
- What do I learn about myself in light of who God is?
- Consider how you fall short of God's character, how the text reveals your sin nature, and what it says about your new identity in Christ.
- How should this truth change me?
- A passage of Scripture may contain direct commands telling us what to do or warnings about sins to avoid in order to help us grow in holiness. Other times, our application flows out of seeing ourselves in light of God's character. As we pray and reflect on how God is calling us to change in light of His Word, we should be asking questions like, "How should I pray for God to change my heart?" and "What practical steps can I take toward cultivating habits of holiness?"

The *Attributes* of God

Eternal
God has no beginning and no end. He always was, always is, and always will be.
HAB. 1:12 / REV. 1:8 / IS. 41:4

Faithful
God is incapable of anything but fidelity. He is loyally devoted to His plan and purpose.
2 TIM. 2:13 / DEUT. 7:9 / HEB. 10:23

Good
God is pure; there is no defilement in Him. He is unable to sin, and all He does is good.
GEN. 1:31 / PS. 34:8 / PS. 107:1

Gracious
God is kind, giving us gifts and benefits we do not deserve.
2 KINGS 13:23 / PS. 145:8
IS. 30:18

Holy
God is undefiled and unable to be in the presence of defilement. He is sacred and set-apart.
REV. 4:8 / LEV. 19:2 / HAB. 1:13

Incomprehensible and Transcendent
God is high above and beyond human understanding. He is unable to be fully known.
PS. 145:3 / IS. 55:8-9
ROM. 11:33-36

Immutable
God does not change. He is the same yesterday, today, and tomorrow.
1 SAM. 15:29 / ROM. 11:29
JAMES 1:17

Infinite
God is limitless. He exhibits all of His attributes perfectly and boundlessly.
ROM. 11:33-36 / IS. 40:28
PS. 147:5

Jealous
God is desirous of receiving the praise and affection He rightly deserves.
EX. 20:5 / DEUT. 4:23-24
JOSH. 24:19

Just
God governs in perfect justice. He acts in accordance with justice. In Him, there is no wrongdoing or dishonesty.
IS. 61:8 / DEUT. 32:4 / PS. 146:7-9

Loving
God is eternally, enduringly, steadfastly loving and affectionate. He does not forsake or betray His covenant love.
JN. 3:16 / EPH. 2:4-5 / 1 JN. 4:16

Merciful
God is compassionate, withholding from us the wrath that we deserve.
TITUS 3:5 / PS. 25:10
LAM. 3:22-23

Omnipotent

God is all-powerful; His strength is unlimited.

MAT. 19:26 / JOB 42:1-2
JER. 32:27

Omnipresent

God is everywhere; His presence is near and permeating.

PROV. 15:3 / PS. 139:7-10
JER. 23:23-24

Omniscient

God is all-knowing; there is nothing unknown to Him.

PS. 147:4 / 1 JN. 3:20
HEB. 4:13

Patient

God is long-suffering and enduring. He gives ample opportunity for people to turn toward Him.

ROM. 2:4 / 2 PET. 3:9 / PS. 86:15

Self-Existent

God was not created but exists by His power alone.

PS. 90:1-2 / JN. 1:4 / JN. 5:26

Self-Sufficient

God has no needs and depends on nothing, but everything depends on God.

IS. 40:28-31 / ACTS 17:24-25
PHIL. 4:19

Sovereign

God governs over all things; He is in complete control.

COL. 1:17 / PS. 24:1-2
1 CHRON. 29:11-12

Truthful

God is our measurement of what is fact. By Him we are able to discern true and false.

JN. 3:33 / ROM. 1:25 / JN. 14:6

Wise

God is infinitely knowledgeable and is judicious with His knowledge.

IS. 46:9-10 / IS. 55:9 / PROV. 3:19

Wrathful

God stands in opposition to all that is evil. He enacts judgment according to His holiness, righteousness, and justice.

PS. 69:24 / JN. 3:36 / ROM. 1:18

Timeline of Scripture

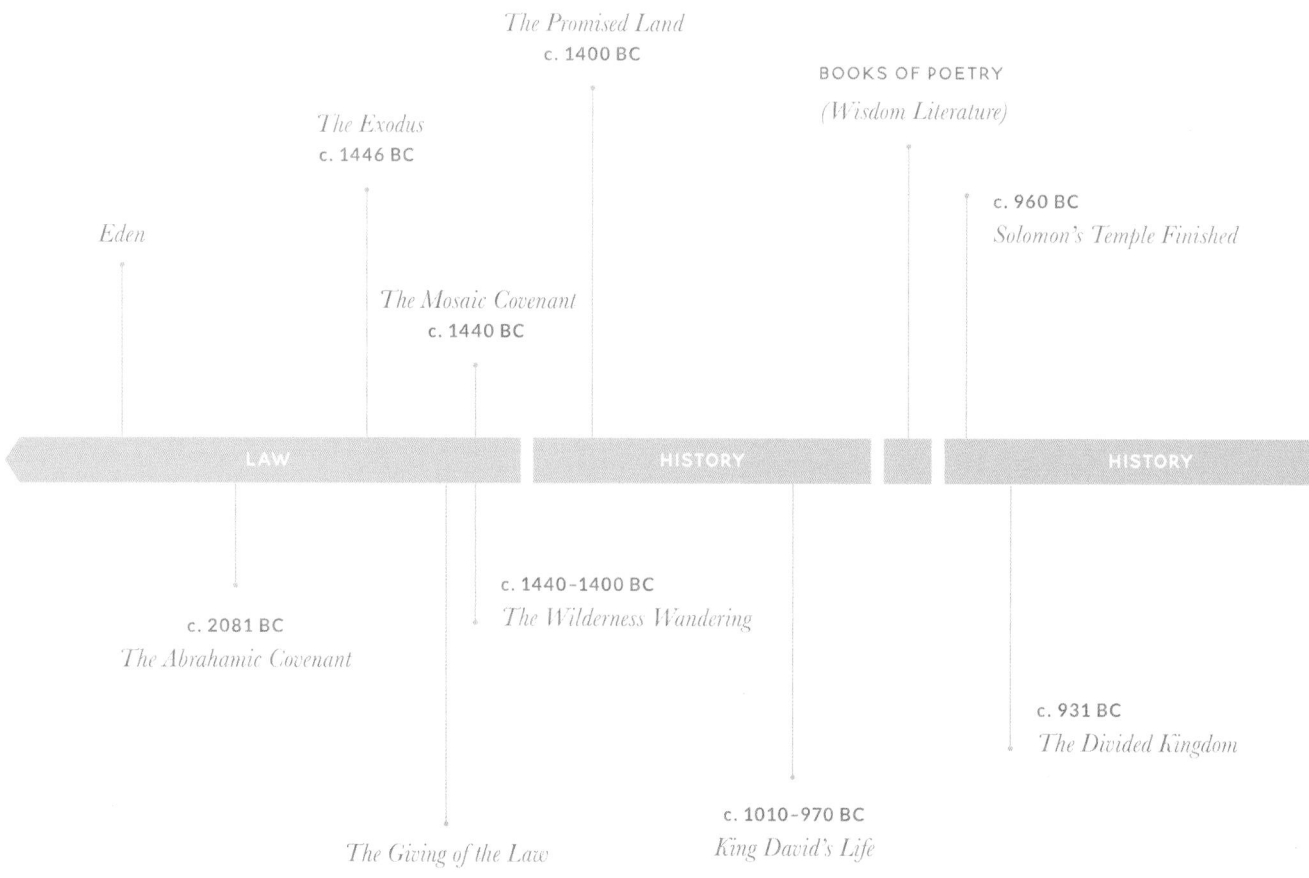

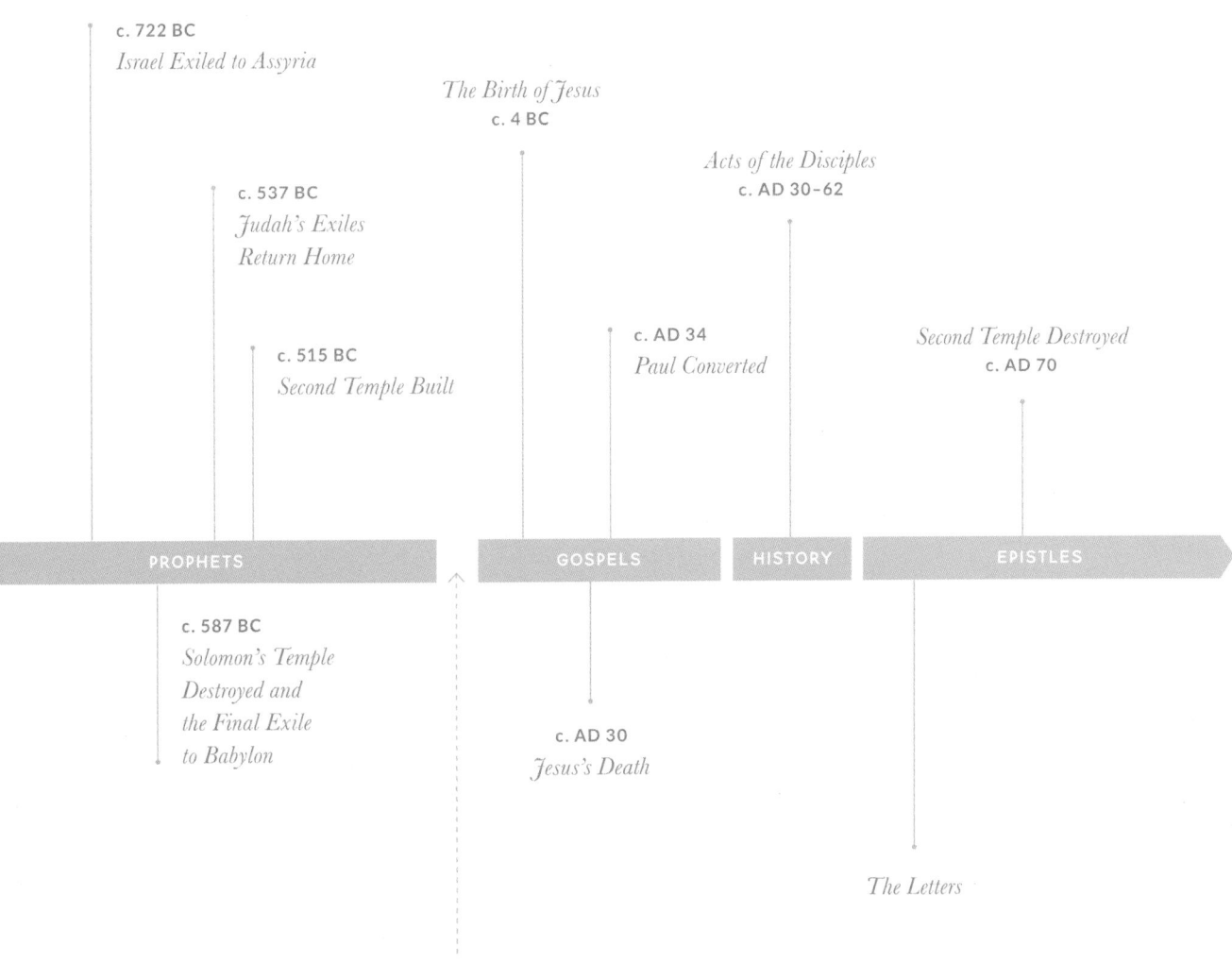

TIMELINE OF SCRIPTURE

Metanarrative of Scripture

Creation

In the beginning, God created the universe. He made the world and everything in it. He created humans in His own image to be His representatives on the earth.

Fall

The first humans, Adam and Eve, disobeyed God by eating from the fruit of the Tree of Knowledge of Good and Evil. Their disobedience impacted the whole world. The punishment for sin is death, and because of Adam's original sin, all humans are sinful and condemned to death.

Redemption

God sent His Son to become a human and redeem His people. Jesus Christ lived a sinless life but died on the cross to pay the penalty for sin. He resurrected from the dead and ascended into heaven. All who put their faith in Jesus are saved from death and freely receive the gift of eternal life.

Restoration

One day, Jesus Christ will return again and restore all that sin destroyed. He will usher in a new heaven and new earth where all who trust in Him will live eternally with glorified bodies in the presence of God.

The gospel is the basis for true relational reconciliation.

THE BOOK OF
Philemon

DATE WRITTEN	c. AD 62
AUTHOR	Paul is the primary author of this letter, though Timothy is also mentioned as a co-sender in verse 1. There is a shift from the plural pronoun "we" in the greeting to the singular pronoun "I" for the rest of the letter. It is likely that Paul wrote this letter during his imprisonment in Rome (Acts 28:30–31).
AUDIENCE	This was a personal letter written to a man named Philemon, a wealthy Christian living in the city of Colossae. Though it was written to him, it was also intended to be read by the Colossian believers who met in Philemon's home. One of Philemon's bondservants, Onesimus, had wronged Philemon in some way and fled to the city of Rome. While there, Onesimus met Paul, became a Christian, and then aided Paul while he was in prison. Paul appeals to Philemon on behalf of Onesimus, hoping that the two may reconcile as brothers in Christ.
HISTORICAL CONTEXT	Colossae was under the rule of the Roman empire at the time Paul wrote this letter. If found, bondservants and slaves who ran away must be returned to their masters. Onesimus was a gift during a difficult season in Paul's life, but Paul knew Onesimus needed to return to Philemon. His return was not just to honor Roman law but to proclaim gospel reconciliation among brothers in Christ to the church.
GENRE	*Epistle*
KEY WORDS	*Restore, Faith, Brother*
THEMES	1. The gospel transforms a Christian's identity and provides restoration. 2. Reconciliation and forgiveness are possible because of Christ's redemptive work on the cross.
KEY VERSE	*For this reason, although I have great boldness in Christ to command you to do what is right, I appeal to you, instead, on the basis of love. I, Paul, as an elderly man and now also as a prisoner of Christ Jesus.* —Philemon 8–9a

Philemon
Practice this week's memory verse.

TUCKED AWAY ON A SINGLE PAGE BETWEEN TITUS AND HEBREWS, THE LETTER TO PHILEMON CAN EASILY BE OVERLOOKED.

As readers, we are dropped into the middle of an ongoing saga involving a master, his runaway slave, and a missionary turned mediator. But as we uncover the context for this letter, we see the beauty of the gospel and its power to restore what is broken.

Paul opens his letter with his typical greeting and words of encouragement. After describing the joy that Philemon's ministry has produced, Paul addresses the issue at hand: there is a broken relationship for Philemon to restore. Paul does not command using harsh words of rebuke but rather appeals to Philemon with love as a brother in Christ.

Paul is asking Philemon to restore his relationship with Onesimus, Philemon's former slave. (It is estimated that almost one-third of those living in the Roman Empire in the first century were considered slaves, primarily living as indentured servants.) Onesimus ran away from Philemon, possibly after committing a crime or stealing from him. While the exact circumstances surrounding this are up for debate, it is clear that something significant caused this fractured relationship with Philemon.

Now Paul is commending Philemon to receive Onesimus because something miraculous has happened. Onesimus met Paul in prison, and as a result, he also met Jesus. Now, as Onesimus's spiritual father, Paul calls Philemon to welcome him back—not as an indentured servant with a checkered past but as a dearly loved brother in Christ (Philemon 16). The gospel is the basis for true relational reconciliation.

In fact, Paul's desire for this reconciliation supersedes his own comfort or support. Onesimus was of great help to him in prison, but Paul knew that Onesimus needed to go back. Thus, Paul offers a way for this relationship to be restored: "And if he has wronged you in any way, or owes you anything, charge that to my account" (Philemon 19). The debt that Onesimus was unable to pay would be paid on his behalf.

This sacrificial mediation should stir our hearts for our own mediator and Savior, Jesus Christ. The gospel restores what was once lost. It redefines our identity, our relationships, and our eternity. The useless is given a purpose. Slaves and masters become brothers in Christ. The sinner is welcomed home. This brief letter is a reminder that the gospel truly restores all that is broken.

Questions

HOW DO YOU SEE THE GOSPEL DISPLAYED IN PAUL'S APPEAL
TO PHILEMON TO WELCOME ONESIMUS BACK?

HOW DOES TODAY'S READING ENCOURAGE YOU TO RUN TO CHRIST
WHEN YOU HAVE SINNED, RATHER THAN RUNNING AWAY?

HOW HAS THE GOSPEL BROUGHT RESTORATION TO YOUR
OWN LIFE, INCLUDING YOUR RELATIONSHIPS?

Jesus is the new and better King. No one compares to Him.

THE BOOK OF
Hebrews

DATE WRITTEN	c. AD 65
AUTHOR	The author of Hebrews is unknown and widely debated. However, many features of this epistle set Hebrews apart—the frequent references to the Old Testament, the emphasis on Jesus's role as High Priest, and the author's formal writing style. The author wrote in more technical Greek than in other New Testament books.
AUDIENCE	The author of Hebrews wrote to Hellenistic Jews within the Roman Empire. These were Greek-speaking Jews who became believers in Christ. These believers were prone to slip into the habits and rituals of Judaism. This letter encourages these Jewish Christians to stand firm in the freedom offered in Christ, our Great High Priest.
HISTORICAL CONTEXT	The author's audience was likely experiencing persecution, and as a result, were mixing Jewish beliefs into their theology of Christ. The author seeks to warn the Hebrews against falling away from Jesus and encourage them with Jesus's superiority over all things—including Jewish tradition.
GENRE	*Epistle*
KEY WORDS	*Priest, Sacrifice, Superior*
THEMES	1. Jesus is our Great High Priest, who fulfilled the Law and provided a once and for all sacrifice on behalf of the sins of His people. 2. Believers are saved into Christ's eternal kingdom by grace through faith in Him. This faith propels Christians to live a life worthy of the grace received from Him.
KEY VERSE	*But Christ has appeared as a high priest of the good things that have come. In the greater and more perfect tabernacle not made with hands (that is, not of this creation), he entered the most holy place once for all time, not by the blood of goats and calves, but by his own blood, having obtained eternal redemption.* —Hebrews 9:1–12

WEEK 41 / DAY 5

Hebrews 1 *Practice this week's memory verse.*

JESUS IS BETTER. HE IS BETTER THAN THE ANGELS.
HE IS BETTER THAN MOSES. HE IS BETTER THAN PROPHETS OF OLD.
HE IS THE NEW AND BETTER SACRIFICE, THE PERFECT PRIEST.

As we start the book of Hebrews today, it is helpful to understand the context of this letter so that we can better understand the author's original meaning. While there is a lot of debate about who wrote the book of Hebrews, we do know that this letter was likely written to a Jewish audience between c. AD 60–70. The letter's audience was facing persecution for their faith (Hebrews 10:32–34) and was in danger of falling away (Hebrews 2:1, 3:12–18). And so, throughout the book of Hebrews, the author encourages his readers to stand firm in the hope of the gospel.

One of the big themes of the book of Hebrews is the supremacy of Christ. Even in chapter 1, the author expresses this theme by talking about the beauty and incomparable worth of Jesus. To do this, the author describes Jesus's nature, characteristics, and works. He explains that Jesus is God's Son, the heir of all things, and the Creator of the world (Hebrews 1:2). He is the radiance of the glory of God—wisdom personified—and His Word has the power to uphold the universe (Hebrews 1:3). He is worshiped by the angels (Hebrews 1:6). His throne is forever and ever, and He is the righteous One (Hebrews 1:8–9). As the author writes about Jesus, he also uses Old Testament references, quoting Psalm 45:6–7, which was originally written about King David. By doing this, the psalmist explains that Jesus is the new and better King. No one compares to Him.

In the past, God spoke to the Israelites through prophets, but in these last days, God has spoken to us through Jesus (Hebrews 1:1). We do not need to be waiting for additional revelation because God has given us everything that we need through His Word and through His Son. Jesus is better than all. He is better than the angels, the Old Testament priests, and the sacrifices. He is better than us, and He is worthy of all praise. Let us worship Him for who He is today.

Throughout the book of Hebrews, the author encourages his readers to stand firm in the hope of the gospel.

Questions

WRITE DOWN A LIST OF JESUS'S ATTRIBUTES AS REFERENCED IN HEBREWS 1.

PICK ONE OF JESUS'S ATTRIBUTES AND STUDY IT. LOOK UP THIS ATTRIBUTE IN THE DICTIONARY AND FIND OTHER VERSES THAT DESCRIBE IT. WRITE THE DEFINITION AND VERSES BELOW.

WEEK 41 / DAY 5

End-of-Week Reflection

Think back on all of the Scripture that you read and studied this week as you answer the questions below.

WHAT DID YOU OBSERVE ABOUT GOD AND HIS CHARACTER?

WHAT DID YOU LEARN ABOUT THE CONDITION OF MANKIND AND YOURSELF?

HOW DOES THIS WEEK'S SCRIPTURE POINT TO THE GOSPEL?

HOW DO THE TRUTHS YOU HAVE LEARNED THIS WEEK ABOUT GOD, MAN, AND THE GOSPEL GIVE YOU HOPE, PEACE, OR ENCOURAGEMENT?

HOW SHOULD YOU RESPOND TO WHAT YOU READ AND LEARNED THIS WEEK?
Write down one or two specific action steps you can take this week to apply what you learned. Then, write a prayer in response to your study of God's Word.

Week Forty-One Application

Before we begin a new week of study, take some time to apply and share the truths of Scripture you learned this week. Here are a few ideas of how you could do this:

- Schedule a meet-up with a friend to share what you are learning from God's Word.
- Use these prompts to journal or pray through what God is revealing to you through your study of His Word.

— LORD, I FEEL…

— LORD, YOU ARE…

— LORD, FORGIVE ME FOR…

— LORD, HELP ME WITH…

- Spend time worshiping God in a way that is meaningful to you, whether that is taking a walk in nature, painting, drawing, singing, etc.

- Paraphrase the Scripture you read this week.

_____
_____
_____
_____
_____
_____
_____
_____
_____
_____
_____
_____

- Use a study Bible or commentary to help you answer questions that came up as you read this week's Scripture.

- Take steps to fulfill the action steps you listed on Day 5.

- Use highlighters to mark the places you see the metanarrative of Scripture in one or more of the passages that you read this week. (See *The Metanarrative of Scripture* on page 14.)

Week Forty-Two Memory Verse

Therefore, since we have a great high priest who has passed through the heavens—Jesus the Son of God—let us hold fast to our confession.

HEBREWS 4:14

WEEK 42 / DAY 1

Hebrews 2 *Practice this week's memory verse.*

JESUS CHRIST IS SUPREME OVER THE ANGELS,
FOR HIS MESSAGE BRINGS SALVATION.

According to Scripture, angels are spiritual beings who serve as God's agents for His kingdom. In yesterday's reading of Hebrews 1, the author explained Christ's superiority over these creatures and highlighted that Jesus is the Creator and heir of all things (Hebrews 1:2). He also described how Jesus, as the eternal Son, bears the exact nature of God, sustains the world, and rules in power and righteousness (Hebrews 1:3, 8–9). The Father has not bestowed such honor to any angel; it is only reserved for His beloved Son.

The author of Hebrews furthers the distinction between Jesus and angels by discussing their messages. For example, angels delivered the Law of God, but Jesus delivered the good news of salvation. According to Deuteronomy 33:2, angels descended with the Lord on Mount Sinai and, upon their Master's command, gave Israel the commands recorded in Leviticus, Numbers, and Deuteronomy (Sproul, 2198). The early Christians believed angels had a role in this event (Acts 7:53, Galatians 3:19) but recognized that the Law did not save them from sin. Instead, they believed that Jesus Christ accomplished salvation and brought not only the message but also the reality of life and forgiveness.

Because Jesus brings greater news, the author warns the reader against refusing to believe (Hebrews 2:2–3). Though angels delivered it, the Law proved to be valid because God held people accountable for defying His commands. Therefore, the gospel is even more valid because Jesus Christ delivered and fulfilled it. So, if we turn from this ultimate message, we will face a punishment most severe.

Though the author acknowledges the Son's superiority over angels, he also explains Jesus's humility. We see this explanation in Hebrews 2:9 when he writes, "But we do see Jesus—made lower than the angels for a short time so that by God's grace he might taste death for everyone—crowned with glory and honor because he suffered death." While not compromising His divinity, the Son of God became a Man, assuming human nature, which is less glorious than the spiritual nature of angels. Jesus humbled Himself so that He could die the punishment we deserved for sin, and because of His perfect obedience and submission, Jesus was raised from the grave. Jesus received the highest honor, bearing more majesty than all of the angels combined.

Questions

HOW WOULD YOU DESCRIBE CHRIST'S SUPREMACY?

WHEN THE SON TOOK ON HUMANITY, HE IDENTIFIED WITH OUR STRUGGLES. HOW DO YOU REACT TO THIS TRUTH?

JESUS IS NOT ASHAMED OF HIS IDENTIFICATION WITH SINFUL HUMANS LIKE US; INSTEAD, HE CALLS US HIS BROTHERS AND SISTERS (HEBREWS 2:12). *How does this familial relationship with Jesus impact your faith journey?*

WEEK 42 / DAY 2

Hebrews 3 *Practice this week's memory verse.*

JESUS IS THE TRUE AND BETTER MOSES; HE DELIVERS US FROM SLAVERY TO SIN AND LEADS US TO GOD'S PROMISED PRESENCE.

Moses was an Old Testament prophet whom God selected to bring the Israelites out of Egyptian slavery. As we see in his story recorded in Exodus, Numbers, and Deuteronomy, Moses was responsible for establishing the nation of Israel in holiness. But Moses was a sinner. He did not complete these duties on his own; the Spirit of God equipped him to deliver the Israelites and point them to truth (Numbers 11:14–17). Through Moses's role, we see a glimpse of the Lord's plan of salvation in Jesus Christ. Moses ultimately points to the One who sets God's people free spiritually and gives them rest in His presence.

The author of Hebrews describes Jesus's fulfillment of Moses's role through the image of a house. For instance, in Hebrews 3:3–4, he writes, "For Jesus is considered worthy of more glory than Moses, just as the builder has more honor than the house. Now every house is built by someone, but the one who built everything is God." Though God called Moses to establish the nation of Israel in holiness, Moses himself was a member of the kingdom like all faithful followers of the Lord. As brick is laid upon a foundation, Moses himself was a part of God's house. He served the Lord, and through his service, God ultimately used him to build up a body of believers.

With Moses as a brick, Jesus is the builder. He is the eternal Son and Creator of all things. Through His Spirit, who applies His saving work to brokenness, Jesus truly builds the kingdom of heaven on earth. He unites His people together—past, present, and future—and builds His Church.

Additionally, the author highlights Jesus's fulfillment through the idea of rest. The Old Testament describes how a generation of Israelites was unable to reach the Promised Land, which was a symbol of rest in God's presence. This was because of their rebellious hearts, as many chose to disobey rather than exercise faith in the Lord. They rejected the Promised Land—this place of rest—and therefore died in the wilderness. Like the Israelites, we deserved this destiny. But Jesus did not leave us to our rebellion. Through His saving work, Jesus set us free from sin. Jesus forgave us of our crimes against the Lord, clearing the debt of corruption. And He led us into true rest through His righteousness.

Questions

HOW DO YOU SEE THE LORD'S FAITHFULNESS IN THIS CHAPTER?

HOW DOES THE RELATIONSHIP BETWEEN MOSES AND JESUS IMPACT YOUR VIEW OF THE OLD TESTAMENT?

HOW DO YOU RESPOND TO THE TRUTH THAT, THROUGH FAITH, YOU ARE A PART OF GOD'S HOUSE?

WEEK 42 / DAY 3

Hebrews 4 *Practice this week's memory verse.*

JESUS GIVES US REST FROM WORLDLY STRIVING AND FROM THE REQUIREMENT OF MORAL PERFECTION TO RECEIVE SALVATION.

In Hebrews 3, we discussed how the Promised Land was a symbol of rest with God. However, the Israelites rejected this place of rest and wanted to go back to Egypt, where they experienced slavery, oppression, and endless toil. Though Egypt brought burdensome labor, the Israelites preferred this work. Their desires reflected the fallen desires of humanity. In our sinful nature, we tend to exchange the Lord's unmerited favor for efforts that bolster our pride and autonomy. However, we are not truly autonomous in these moments. Instead, like the Israelites, we chain ourselves to sin and try to carry the weight of God's law without any ability to keep it.

But still, the Lord wanted His people to experience rest. He wanted to give us much better than what we desired for ourselves. So, the Father sent a gift that we could not exchange: He sent Jesus Christ. When Jesus arrived, He lived a life of moral perfection. His righteousness exceeded the requirement of keeping the Law for salvation. Through faith in Jesus's saving work, we are free from this requirement and receive God's unmerited favor, for Jesus covers us in His righteousness and shares His reward of eternal life. Therefore, we can let go of meaningless efforts to obtain worldly success. We can abandon attempts to prove ourselves worthy. And we can truly rest in Christ.

Additionally, the author of Hebrews describes what the rest God offers us is like through the Sabbath. The Sabbath was a day when the Israelites had to cease their labor. On this day, the Israelites mirrored the moment when God rested from creating the universe (Hebrews 4:4). In this way, the Sabbath rest invited the Israelites to experience the delight the Lord had when He completed His work. The saving work of Jesus allows all believers to enter Sabbath rest by leading us into the delightful presence of God.

Furthermore, the author claims the Sabbath rest is eternal. For instance, he writes, "Therefore, a Sabbath rest remains for God's people. For the person who has entered his rest has rested from his own works, just as God did from his" (Hebrews 4:9–10). Though God sustains the processes of nature that He established at creation, God is no longer creating new universes. He now enjoys the fruits of His labor and will do so for eternity. Likewise, in Christ, rest is not limited to a day. Because of Jesus's accomplishment, we can enter the rest of God forever and at all times.

Questions

HOW DOES HEBREWS 4:11 ENCOURAGE YOU TO BE FAITHFUL TO THE LORD IN RESPONSE TO THE GIFT OF SALVATION?

THE AUTHOR OF HEBREWS OFTEN QUOTES FROM OTHER VERSES OF SCRIPTURE AS HE EXPLAINS THE ROLE OF JESUS. *How does this help you understand the way the entire Bible works together to tell one story?*

IN WHAT AREAS CAN YOU EXPERIENCE MORE REST IN CHRIST?

WEEK 42 / DAY 4

Hebrews 5 *Practice this week's memory verse.*

JESUS IS THE TRUE HIGH PRIEST, WHO UNDERSTANDS OUR WEAKNESSES, REPRESENTS US BEFORE GOD'S THRONE, AND BRIDGES THE GAP BETWEEN US AND THE FATHER.

In the Old Testament, the priests were responsible for leading Israel in right worship. They taught the Law and offered animal sacrifices to pay for the people's sins. The high priest was selected to enter the Holy of Holies once a year. The Holy of Holies was the innermost part of God's earthly dwelling place, which was first in the tabernacle and later in the temple, and it was there that the Spirit of God rested. On the Day of Atonement (which was one of Israel's holidays), the high priest came before the Spirit of God and presented an offering to pay for the entire community's sins for that year.

Ultimately, the role of the priests was a picture of the saving work Jesus accomplished. The priests themselves were sinners and could not offer payment that would completely satisfy divine justice. But, as the perfect Son of God, Jesus offered Himself as payment. Jesus fulfilled the priesthood, providing the ultimate sacrifice and giving us access to the holy presence of God.

We can understand Jesus's role as our mediator through the lens of a defense lawyer. A defense lawyer is someone who advocates for an accused criminal. The lawyer defends him or her against the prosecution's claims and seeks mercy from the judge. We can see Jesus in this light as He advocates for us in heaven's courtroom, rebukes Satan's accusations, and provides His death as payment so that we receive mercy. However, Jesus stands apart from defense lawyers with His empathy. Jesus truly knows the temptations we face in this broken world. Furthermore, though not sinning Himself, Jesus bore the weight of our past, present, and future sins, suffering our punishment for those crimes.

Lastly, Jesus serves as High Priest for eternity. The author of Hebrews indicates this truth in Hebrews 5:5–6 when he writes, "In the same way, Christ did not exalt himself to become a high priest, but God who said to him, 'You are my Son; today I have become your Father,' also says in another place, 'You are a priest forever according to the order of Melchizedek.'" Jesus's eternal priesthood brings us comfort when we fail. Through faith in Christ, we know that we always have an advocate. Jesus's blood will never lose its power, and His righteousness will not cease to cover our sin.

Questions

HOW DOES THE ROLE OF THE PRIESTS ILLUMINATE YOUR NEED FOR CHRIST?

HOW SHOULD YOU RESPOND TO THE TRUTH THAT JESUS IS YOUR ADVOCATE?

IN HEBREWS 5:11–14, THE AUTHOR OF HEBREWS EMPHASIZES THE IMPORTANCE OF SPIRITUAL MATURITY. WRITE A PRAYER THAT ASKS GOD FOR A MATURE FAITH THAT SEEKS TO KNOW GOD AND HIS WORD.

WEEK 42 / DAY 5

Hebrews 6 *Practice this week's memory verse.*

YOU HAVE LIKELY SEEN HEBREWS 6:19 SCRIPTED ACROSS WALL DECOR AND DECORATIVE PILLOWS: "WE HAVE THIS HOPE AS AN ANCHOR FOR THE SOUL, FIRM AND SECURE."

Though this verse is beautiful on the surface, it is even more stunning in the context of this passage. In Hebrews 6, the author warns against apostasy, or falling away from the faith. Just as an infant matures from drinking milk to eating solid food, believers should be continuously maturing in their faith, moving from foundational knowledge to faith in action.

To warn of the dangers of apostasy, Hebrews presents a humbling illustration. The author describes a person who receives good gospel teaching, who has seen the Holy Spirit at work, and who has tasted or benefited from the good fruit of the church. However, this person, even after hearing and experiencing the truth of God's Word, still vehemently rejects Him. For this person—for the stubborn-hearted denier of Jesus—there is no hope of repentance nor reward in heaven. Though they sat among the saved, they did not come to true saving faith themselves. Though they may have trusted in Christ for a season, their lack of perseverance showcases a lack of saving faith. It is as if this person crucifies Jesus again (Hebrews 6:6). Yes, this example is extreme, but it wakes the drowsy Christian to action. Our hope in Christ is more than a pretty quote upon a pillow; it is the pathway to life, the assurance of our salvation.

As if the author knows that this example will stun his audience, he encourages them that their faith rests secure. God knows their hearts and sees their sacrifices. He will complete the good work that He began in them by the grace of His Son, Jesus. And God cannot break His promises.

The author then turns the audience's attention to Abraham, known as the father of faith. Abraham trusted God to provide him a son, even in his old age—a faith that set forth God's plan to redeem the world through Jesus. God was faithful to provide Abraham's son, Isaac (Genesis 21), and He was faithful to provide a Messiah, a Savior to wash our sins away. If He was faithful then, surely He will be faithful to welcome His children into heaven at the end of our days. God's faithfulness is the hope upon which our souls anchor. It is the truth that keeps us afloat on our worst days and the song we sing from the mountaintop on our best.

Questions

THIS PASSAGE SPEAKS OF ASSURANCE FOR THOSE IN CHRIST WHO PERSEVERE. MANY THEOLOGIANS CALL THIS IDEA "PERSEVERANCE OF THE SAINTS." READ EPHESIANS 1:13–14 AND PHILIPPIANS 1:6. *What do these verses teach you about the security of salvation for those who trust in Christ?*

THIS PASSAGE ENCOURAGES US TO REMAIN ACTIVE IN OUR FAITH. READ HEBREWS 6:11–12. IF YOU ARE HONEST, IN WHAT AREAS OF YOUR FAITH HAVE YOU BEEN LAZY OR NEGLECTFUL? *Write them below. Spend time in prayer, asking for God's forgiveness and His wisdom to help you put your faith into action.*

WEEK 42 / DAY 5

End-of-Week Reflection

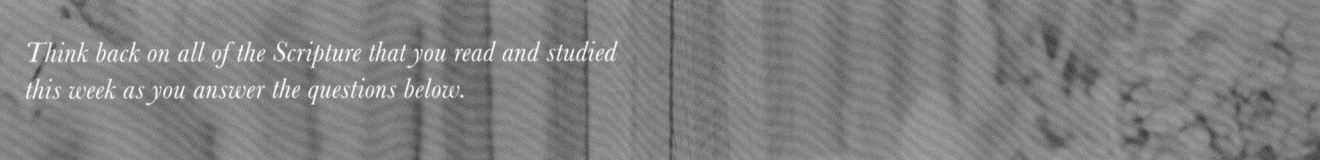

Think back on all of the Scripture that you read and studied this week as you answer the questions below.

WHAT DID YOU OBSERVE ABOUT GOD AND HIS CHARACTER?

WHAT DID YOU LEARN ABOUT THE CONDITION OF MANKIND AND YOURSELF?

HOW DOES THIS WEEK'S SCRIPTURE POINT TO THE GOSPEL?

HOW DO THE TRUTHS YOU HAVE LEARNED THIS WEEK ABOUT GOD, MAN, AND THE GOSPEL GIVE YOU HOPE, PEACE, OR ENCOURAGEMENT?

HOW SHOULD YOU RESPOND TO WHAT YOU READ AND LEARNED THIS WEEK?
Write down one or two specific action steps you can take this week to apply what you learned. Then, write a prayer in response to your study of God's Word.

Week Forty-Two Application

Before we begin a new week of study, take some time to apply and share the truths of Scripture you learned this week. Here are a few ideas of how you could do this:

- Schedule a meet-up with a friend to share what you are learning from God's Word.
- Use these prompts to journal or pray through what God is revealing to you through your study of His Word.

— LORD, I FEEL…

— LORD, YOU ARE…

— LORD, FORGIVE ME FOR…

— LORD, HELP ME WITH…

- Spend time worshiping God in a way that is meaningful to you, whether that is taking a walk in nature, painting, drawing, singing, etc.

- Paraphrase the Scripture you read this week.

_____
_____
_____
_____
_____
_____
_____
_____
_____
_____
_____
_____
_____

- Use a study Bible or commentary to help you answer questions that came up as you read this week's Scripture.

- Take steps to fulfill the action steps you listed on Day 5.

- Use highlighters to mark the places you see the metanarrative of Scripture in one or more of the passages that you read this week. (See *The Metanarrative of Scripture* on page 14.)

Week Forty-Three Memory Verse

Now faith is the reality of what is hoped for, the proof of what is not seen.

HEBREWS 11:1

WEEK 43 / DAY 1

Hebrews 7 *Practice this week's memory verse.*

SCRIPTURE USES SEVERAL NAMES TO DESCRIBE JESUS: SAVIOR, SON OF GOD, SON OF MAN, REDEEMER, AND MANY MORE.

But perhaps the most difficult to understand is the Great High Priest, which is first referenced in Hebrews 4. Hebrews 6 even closes by calling Jesus the "high priest forever according to the order of Melchizedek."

You may be wondering, *Who is Melchizedek?* Hebrews 7 explains who he is. Melchizedek is mentioned in three books of the Bible: Genesis 14:18–20, Psalm 110:4, and here in Hebrews. In Genesis 14, Abram (later known as Abraham) rescues his nephew Lot from captivity, and on the way back home, he meets Melchizedek. This man was both king and priest of Salem (ancient Jerusalem). Melchizedek was so revered that Abraham gave him a tenth of his victories (Hebrews 7:4). In order to help his Jewish audience best understand Christ's roles as Great High Priest and King of kings, the author of Hebrews uses Melchizedek—an example from their history who also held these dual roles.

In Jewish culture, the idea of being both a priest and a king is almost unheard of, as priests and kings are appointed from different tribes. God appointed the priests to come from the tribe of Levi (Exodus 28:1–4) and the kings to come from the tribe of Judah (Genesis 49:10). However, there are two people in Jewish history who simultaneously held both roles: Melchizedek and Jesus. Melchizedek's reign as priest and king occurred before God established the laws for the nation of Israel, making him the only priest/king until the arrival of Jesus. Though Jesus hails from the tribe of Judah, He holds dual roles because He is the final priest—the One who accomplishes all priestly duties in Himself. Jesus, being perfectly sinless, is the only man qualified to be a spotless lamb worthy of sacrifice to God (Hebrews 7:27). God satisfies His own wrath against sin by the blood of His blameless Son.

In Psalm 110:4, the Lord promises Israel another priest, a priest who will one day serve forever and follow in the likeness of Melchizedek. In Hebrews 7, the author connects this promise to Jesus (Hebrews 7:17). God exchanged the temporary system of Levitical priests, which was marred by sin and corruption, for a final solution for sin—a final sacrifice. Now, Christ reigns as the eternal Priest and eternal King, whose blood covers the sins of God's people. Jesus is the fulfillment of this promise. Melchizedek was a man whom God used to communicate this future redemption of His people. With only three mentions of him in the Bible, the life of Melchizedek remains somewhat of a mystery. However, his legacy is not. Melchizedek foreshadows the King and Priest to come—the Savior, through whom all are blessed.

Questions

BEFORE TODAY'S READING, HAD YOU EVER HEARD OF MELCHIZEDEK? HOW DOES TODAY'S PASSAGE HELP YOU UNDERSTAND HOW ALL OF SCRIPTURE POINTS TO JESUS?

HOW DOES JESUS PERFECTLY MEET THE ROLES OF GREAT HIGH PRIEST AND KING OF KINGS? FOR HELP ANSWERING THIS QUESTION, CONSIDER READING ISAIAH 9:6–7, PHILIPPIANS 2:7–8, AND HEBREWS 4:14–16.

COMPARE JESUS WITH THE PRIESTS OF THE OLD COVENANT. HOW IS JESUS BETTER? WHY DO WE NO LONGER NEED ANOTHER PRIEST? (HINT: READ HEBREWS 7:23–28.)

WEEK 43 / DAY 2

Hebrews 8 *Practice this week's memory verse.*

A THESIS STATEMENT SERVES AS AN ANCHOR FOR A WRITTEN PIECE. ALL OTHER SENTENCES IN THAT PIECE ARE MADE TO SUPPORT AND CONFIRM THE THESIS: THE ESSENTIAL MAIN POINT.

In Hebrews 8, the author makes his thesis statement for this chapter of Hebrews clear: Jesus is the Great High Priest—chosen as the full and final sacrifice for sin (Hebrews 8:1). Jesus is not like priests on earth, qualified only by familial lineage to serve in temporary tabernacles. Jesus was appointed by God Himself to serve in a tabernacle that is permanently established in heaven.

To best understand this chapter, let us remind ourselves of the tabernacle (Exodus 25–31). Even though the Israelites continuously rebelled against God, He created a way for His presence to dwell among them. The tabernacle is the structure that held God's presence among the Israelite community. God gave specific details for its construction and for the sacrifices made to cleanse the people from their sin.

Sin is costly and requires the blood of several choice animals. This blood temporarily covered the cost of sin. But in Hebrews 8, we learn that sacrifices and the tabernacle were only a shadow of what was to come. Now, the true and lasting tabernacle is in heaven, where Jesus's sacrifice fully satisfies the wrath of God. Because of the cross, nothing separates us from God. For those who trust in Jesus for salvation, God's presence dwells richly through the Holy Spirit.

Not only is Jesus the better, all-sufficient sacrifice, but He ushers forth a better law. The author of Hebrews quotes Jeremiah 31:31–34 to illustrate this point. God spoke through Jeremiah, a prophet of God, to promise a future hope for Israel. This hope, long foretold to God's people, served as a reminder in the darkest days of their history that God does not forget His children. This covenant is confirmed and revealed in Jesus. Christ is the promise kept.

Through Jesus, we are sealed under a new, unbreakable covenant—one that is not dependent on our faithfulness but on Jesus's perfect obedience. God gave the original Law to Moses as a taste of His glory to come. Through Jesus, our hope is secure, and we have no division between us and God's presence.

Questions

COUNT THE NUMBER OF TIMES THAT THE WORD "COVENANT" IS REPEATED IN THIS CHAPTER. WHY MIGHT THE AUTHOR OF HEBREWS USE THIS WORD TO DESCRIBE JESUS'S NEW MINISTRY AND REIGN AS THE GREAT HIGH PRIEST?

READ 1 CORINTHIANS 3:16–17. UNDER THE NEW COVENANT, GOD'S TEMPLE IS THE BODY OF EVERY BELIEVER; THEREFORE, HIS PRESENCE NEVER LEAVES HIS PEOPLE. HOW DOES THIS TRUTH DIFFER FROM THE DAYS OF THE TABERNACLE?

RIGHT NOW, IF YOU ARE READING THIS AS A BELIEVER, GOD'S PRESENCE DWELLS RICHLY WITH YOU. IT IS EASY TO TAKE THIS GIFT FOR GRANTED. *Write a prayer of thanksgiving, praising God for never leaving and forsaking you.*

WEEK 43 / DAY 3

Hebrews 9 *Practice this week's memory verse.*

ONCE AND FOR ALL. CHRIST'S SACRIFICE WAS ENOUGH
TO SATISFY GOD'S WRATH IN FULL.

No other sacrifice, no other tabernacle, no other ritual is needed to secure the forgiveness of sins. Jesus is enough. This is the theme that weaves together Hebrews 9. In this chapter, the author compares and contrasts the old covenant, brought forth through Moses, with the new covenant, inaugurated by Christ. The Mosaic covenant included the Ten Commandments, moral and civil laws, and laws that outlined the specific way that the Israelites were to enter God's presence.

As we discussed yesterday, the tabernacle was a holy tent that the Israelite priests entered to commune with God and offer sacrifices for the forgiveness of sin. The tent was separated into two parts, the Holy Place and the Most Holy Place. The Holy Place was entered into by any priest and was attended to regularly. However, the Most Holy Place was only visited once each year by the high priest on the Day of Atonement when Israel's sin was paid for through a blood sacrifice. Any other person entering the Most Holy Place would die in the presence of God. At the appropriate time, the high priest would offer sacrifices to atone for the sins of himself and the Israelite community. However, the tabernacle was a temporary solution to an eternal problem. Sin still ran rampant throughout Israel. The Israelites still forgot God. Eternal problems must be solved with eternal solutions.

Hebrews 9 tells us that this system was merely a placeholder for the Great High Priest to come. Jesus establishes a new and better covenant. He is the Great High Priest, who enters the Most Holy Place—the presence of God—and sacrifices Himself to atone for the sins of mankind now and forevermore. In fact, in the CSB translation, the word "blood" is referenced twelve times in these twenty-eight verses. While the blood of goats and rams temporarily forgave sins, Christ's blood proves the eternal solution. Jesus abolished the need for the Mosaic tabernacle and temple in Jerusalem. He completed all priestly duties in the holiest of holy places, the throne of God in heaven.

Why can we trust this covenant? Because the old covenant was sealed with the sprinkling of the blood of livestock. But this new covenant is sealed by the very blood of Jesus. His sinlessness secures our cleanliness. His humility secured our freedom, once and for all.

Questions

COMPARE AND CONTRAST THE OLD COVENANT WITH
THE NEW COVENANT, AS DESCRIBED IN HEBREWS 9.

Old Covenant	*New Covenant*

READ LEVITICUS 17:11, HEBREWS 9:22, AND EPHESIANS 1:7.
WHY IS BLOOD NEEDED TO ATONE FOR SINS? WHY IS JESUS'S BLOOD THE
ONLY BLOOD THAT CAN ATONE FOR THE SINS OF ALL OF GOD'S PEOPLE?

BLOOD IS NOT SPILLED WITHOUT PAIN. TAKE A MOMENT TO REFLECT ON
MATTHEW 26:36–42. JESUS FELT SORROW IN ANTICIPATION OF HIS DEATH.
Write a prayer below, thanking Jesus for His humility and willingness to suffer on our behalf.

WEEK 43 / DAY 4

Hebrews 10 *Practice this week's memory verse.*

IN TODAY'S READING, THE AUTHOR CONTINUES TO BUILD UPON AN OVERARCHING THEME IN HEBREWS: JESUS IS SUFFICIENT.

As you read, chapter 10 may feel a bit repetitive. Throughout chapters 8–10, the author of Hebrews continually solidifies an argument that secures Jesus Christ as the better—the only—sacrifice needed to atone for sins.

Yesterday, we learned that Israelite priests would perform sacrifices on behalf of God's people on a yearly basis. Yet these sacrifices under the Mosaic Covenant were temporary and insufficient. However, scholars believe that some Christian believers of the time were combining Jewish traditions with Christian beliefs. Therefore, the author emphasizes that nothing can be added to Jesus. In fact, throughout Hebrews 9 and 10, the phrases "once for all time" or "once and for all" are repeated three times (Hebrews 9:12, 10:2, 10:10). Through this repetition, the author of Hebrews dismantles the need for the Old Testament sacrificial system. Jesus is the greater sacrifice, the final sacrificial lamb.

Even from far before Jesus's time, it was made known to the Israelites that the sacrifices of bulls and goats did not fully satisfy God's wrath against sin, for these sacrifices had to be made over and over again, year after year. Therefore, there was a regular remembrance of and sacrifice for sin among the Israelite community. But in the new covenant, Jesus wipes our slate clean once and for all to secure a deeper relationship between God and His children. Since the beginning of time, God has wanted the hearts of His people—a deep, everyday worship that leads to obedience. Jesus freed us from the bondage of sin so that we can instead draw near to God. We cannot make Him think less of us, nor can we earn our place near His throne. Jesus secured for us what no man and no sacrifice could—the permanent forgiveness of sin. Grace upon grace.

And because this grace is secure, any man or woman who trusts in Jesus as their Savior can draw near to God. We do not need to be priests; we do not need to be perfect. In all our messiness, we can approach the throne of God without fear, for when He sees us, He remembers His Son. This privilege is our badge of honor, the rock upon which we stand secure, for we know that He who promised our salvation is faithful (Hebrews 10:23). This grace propels us to devote our lives to the gospel so that the world may know that Jesus is Lord.

Questions

READ HOSEA 6:6 AND PSALM 51:16–17. EVEN IN THE OLD TESTAMENT, WHAT DID GOD VALUE MORE THAN SACRIFICES? HOW DOES JESUS FULFILL GOD'S ULTIMATE DESIRE?

IN LIGHT OF JESUS'S SACRIFICE AND OUR ASSURANCE OF FAITH, HEBREWS 10 CALLS US TO LIVE IN LIGHT OF OUR SALVATION. TAKE A LOOK AT HEBREWS 10:19–25. *How might you better pursue godliness according to these verses?*

AT THE END OF CHAPTER 10, THE AUTHOR OF HEBREWS WARNS AGAINST DELIBERATE SIN. DO YOU HAVE ANY SINS YOU ARE CURRENTLY COMMITTING THAT YOU HAVE NOT BROUGHT BEFORE GOD? *If so, take time to write a prayer of repentance in the space below. A prayer of repentance laments over sin, acknowledges that it is wrong, and then vows to turn from the sinful pattern. For inspiration, read Psalm 51.*

WEEK 43 / DAY 5

Hebrews 11 *Practice this week's memory verse.*

THE OLD TESTAMENT IS FULL OF PEOPLE WHO ARE REGARDED FOR THEIR FAITH.

Although none of them were perfect, they trusted God, and God worked through them to accomplish His purposes. Like walking down a hall and looking at portraits of important figures, the author of Hebrews walks us through the "heroes" of the faith in the Old Testament. In doing so, the author encourages his readers—and us—to have faith in the God who works wonders throughout history.

Before diving into the faithful saints of old, the author first describes what faith is: "faith is the reality of what is hoped for, the proof of what is not seen" (Hebrews 11:1). In other words, faith is trusting in what is unseen. But faith is not blind. For the believer, faith involves believing and clinging to who they know to be true—God. To demonstrate this truth, the author of Hebrews describes how prominent people in the Old Testament placed their faith in a God they could not see because they knew He was trustworthy and true.

Through the testimony of one of these saints, Enoch, we receive an important lesson. Without faith, we cannot please God (Hebrews 11:6). In order to have a relationship with God, we must believe that God is who He says He is. While there is more we must believe, someone cannot expect to be approved by God if he does not believe in God.

As we journey through Hebrews 11, we receive examples of how faith involves trusting in the unseen. For example, Noah was warned about a flood that he could not see, yet his fear of the Lord led him to trust God. Abraham left his home, even though he could not see where he was going, because he trusted God. Rather than focusing on temporary dwellings, Abraham focused on the eternal home God was building.

The faith of these figures is encouraging, but what is startling is that these people did not receive what was ultimately promised. They saw God's immediate promises fulfilled, but they did not see His promise of a Messiah fulfilled. Even still, they trusted. How much more should we trust the God who has given us His Son? We know from God's Word that Christ has come and will return. So let us, too, look ahead to what is to come—even though we cannot see it—and trust our God, whose faithfulness stands the test of time.

Questions

WHICH PERSON'S TESTIMONY IN HEBREWS 11
STANDS OUT THE MOST TO YOU AND WHY?

WHY IS GOD TRUSTWORTHY? HOW IS OUR FAITH
MOTIVATED BY WHO HE IS AND WHAT HE DOES?

WEEK 43 / DAY 5

End-of-Week Reflection

Think back on all of the Scripture that you read and studied this week as you answer the questions below.

WHAT DID YOU OBSERVE ABOUT GOD AND HIS CHARACTER?

WHAT DID YOU LEARN ABOUT THE CONDITION OF MANKIND AND YOURSELF?

HOW DOES THIS WEEK'S SCRIPTURE POINT TO THE GOSPEL?

HOW DO THE TRUTHS YOU HAVE LEARNED THIS WEEK ABOUT GOD, MAN, AND THE GOSPEL GIVE YOU HOPE, PEACE, OR ENCOURAGEMENT?

HOW SHOULD YOU RESPOND TO WHAT YOU READ AND LEARNED THIS WEEK?
Write down one or two specific action steps you can take this week to apply what you learned. Then, write a prayer in response to your study of God's Word.

Week Forty-Three Application

Before we begin a new week of study, take some time to apply and share the truths of Scripture you learned this week. Here are a few ideas of how you could do this:

- Schedule a meet-up with a friend to share what you are learning from God's Word.
- Use these prompts to journal or pray through what God is revealing to you through your study of His Word.

— LORD, I FEEL…

— LORD, YOU ARE…

— LORD, FORGIVE ME FOR…

— LORD, HELP ME WITH…

- Spend time worshiping God in a way that is meaningful to you, whether that is taking a walk in nature, painting, drawing, singing, etc.

- Paraphrase the Scripture you read this week.

_____
_____
_____
_____
_____
_____
_____
_____
_____
_____
_____
_____
_____
_____

- Use a study Bible or commentary to help you answer questions that came up as you read this week's Scripture.

- Take steps to fulfill the action steps you listed on Day 5.

- Use highlighters to mark the places you see the metanarrative of Scripture in one or more of the passages that you read this week. (See *The Metanarrative of Scripture* on page 14.)

Week Forty-Four Memory Verse

Jesus Christ is the same yesterday, today, and forever.

HEBREWS 13:8

WEEK 44 / DAY 1

Hebrews 12 *Practice this week's memory verse.*

THE AUTHOR OF HEBREWS HAS GIVEN HIS READERS TESTIMONIES OF FAITHFUL SAINTS IN HEBREWS 11.

Now, he returns to address the readers directly. Though these testimonies are great, they are testimonies of people from the past. The present remains difficult, and believers must persevere as they face suffering. In Hebrews 12, the author gives his readers hope in the midst of affliction. Though they experience trouble, they can have endurance because of the One who goes before them and is with them.

In verses 1–2, the author uses the imagery of a race. He compares his readers to runners who are racing toward eternity while the faithful saints of old watch on as spectators. Yet, although these saints are spectators, their faithful examples serve to encourage the believers to run with endurance. In order to run effectively, the readers must put off the sin that distracts them and weighs them down. And even though the testimonies of the faithful saints in the Old Testament are fuel for endurance, there is an even greater motivation for endurance—Jesus. Jesus demonstrated endurance during His time on earth by going to the cross. Even though His fate was death, Jesus joyfully took on the cross so that we could be saved. Christ's endurance on the cross motivates our own. As we run the Christian race, we do so with our gaze fixed on Christ, the One who has given us faith and is perfecting our faith.

As we have discussed, the author is writing to believers who are experiencing suffering. Yet their suffering does not compare to Christ's. Jesus's suffering involved shedding His blood for us. Though we might not experience that level of suffering, we will still experience trials and troubles in this life. What hope do we have in the midst of suffering? We can trust that God is using our suffering for our sanctification.

In verses 5–11, the author describes God's discipline. Just as a father disciplines his children for their good, so does God discipline us as His children for our good. Likewise, just as the discipline of running is painful at first until it yields results, so is the discipline we receive from God painful until it yields the holiness that God's discipline produces. While suffering is difficult, we can endure it, knowing that God is using our suffering to make us holy. Running the Christian race will involve hardship, but we can persevere—not only as we look to Christ but also as we look ahead to our completed sanctification.

Questions

WHAT HINDRANCES AND SINS DO YOU NEED TO LAY ASIDE SO THAT YOU CAN RUN THE RACE OF THE CHRISTIAN LIFE WELL?

HOW DO GOD'S CHARACTER AND PURPOSES HELP YOU RECEIVE RATHER THAN REJECT HIS DISCIPLINE?

HOW DO VERSES 18–28 DESCRIBE OUR ACCESS TO GOD AS BELIEVERS? HOW DOES OUR ACCESS TO GOD AND THE UNSHAKEABLE KINGDOM THAT WE ARE MEMBERS OF ENCOURAGE YOUR GRATITUDE AND WORSHIP?

WEEK 44 / DAY 2

Hebrews 13 *Practice this week's memory verse.*

EVERY LETTER MUST COME TO A CLOSE, AND IT IS NOW TIME FOR THIS LETTER TO THE HEBREWS TO FINISH.

As the author closes, he leaves his readers with some final encouragement. In fact, this closing portion summarizes all that the author has been trying to communicate to his readers. Hebrews 13 gives the author's original readers—and all of us as believers—wisdom and encouragement to live the Christian life well.

The author first writes a series of exhortations in a rapid-fire fashion. The majority of the exhortations in verses 1–8 have to do with our treatment of one another. As followers of Christ, we are to be people of brotherly love and hospitality. We are to consider and pray for those who are imprisoned and afflicted. Our marriages should be honorable and pure. Believers are also to respect and listen to their leaders. We are to remember, obey, and submit to our leaders. But we are also to observe how they live their lives and imitate their faith.

The author also includes exhortations in this chapter that do not pertain to others directly. In verse 8, the author reminds his readers of the constancy of Christ. Jesus remains the same no matter what. Therefore, He can be trusted. Because Jesus does not change, we can cling to Him with confidence. But the constancy of Christ also influences our actions as believers. We reflect the God who does not change by being people who pursue consistent faithfulness to the Lord.

In verse 9, the author warns his readers not to be led astray by strange teachings. He specifically references one that has to do with food regulations. It seems as if some people are treating food as more important and necessary than God's grace. While food is needed for the body, we are ultimately to be dependent on God's grace. The author illustrates this truth by reminding his readers of Christ's sacrifice. Similar to sacrifices that were burned outside the camp, so did Jesus suffer outside the gate of Jerusalem on the cross. As believers, we spiritually join Jesus outside the "camp" by allowing ourselves to suffer for Christ's sake. We live the Christian life by reflecting our Savior through our actions and in our sufferings, looking ahead to our inheritance to come, and, through the power of the Spirit, depending on the grace of our God, who never leaves us or forsakes us.

Questions

REREAD HEBREWS 13:5–6. HOW DOES GOD'S CHARACTER KEEP US FROM LOVING MONEY?

HOW DOES THE GOOD NEWS OF THE GOSPEL MOTIVATE US TO OFFER UP SACRIFICES OF PRAISE TO GOD? WHAT DOES THIS LOOK LIKE PRACTICALLY?

REREAD HEBREWS 13:20–21. HOW DO THESE VERSES COMFORT AND ENCOURAGE YOU AS YOU LIVE THE CHRISTIAN LIFE?

We can endure through suffering because by doing so, we are following in our Savior's footsteps.

THE BOOK OF
James

DATE WRITTEN	c. AD 45–50
AUTHOR	James, the half-brother of Jesus, wrote this letter (Matthew 13:55). James denied Jesus as Messiah at first (Mark 3:21–25) but later came to saving faith in Christ. Additionally, he became a wise leader of the church in Jerusalem (Acts 15:13–17), earning him the title "James the Just" among the Jews. This letter is a summary of Christ-centered theology and wisdom.
AUDIENCE	Unlike Paul's letters, which are written for a specific person or church, this letter is intended for the wider audience of Jewish Christians of the Diaspora (James 1:1). These were Jews who were no longer in Israel and were scattered throughout Europe and Asia. Because of this, James did not address any specific situations or people but instead spoke of how all Christians should live.
HISTORICAL CONTEXT	James addressed believers living under Roman rule. Rome believed in the freedom to live however you please and feared no consequences for their sinful choices. James spoke to Christians about the practical steps they can take to live a life that displays Christ and does not give in to the carnal desires of the world around them.
GENRE	*Epistle*
KEY WORDS	*Faith, Works, Wisdom*
THEMES	1. Christ-followers should live wisely by devoting themselves to the teachings of Christ. 2. The faith of believers should result in good works through the Spirit working within them.
KEY VERSE	*For just as the body without the spirit is dead, so also faith without works is dead.* —James 2:26

WEEK 44 / DAY 3

James 1
Practice this week's memory verse.

HAVE YOU EVER RECEIVED A GREAT PIECE OF ADVICE? IN THE BOOK OF JAMES, JAMES SHARES PRACTICAL WISDOM WITH JEWISH CHRISTIANS OR JEWISH CONVERTS SCATTERED OUTSIDE THE LAND OF ISRAEL.

Once a skeptic, James (the half-brother of Jesus) came to faith after Jesus's death and resurrection, and he grew to be a leader of the Christian church in Jerusalem. As an extension of his ministry, James writes this letter to Jewish Christians to encourage them in practical obedience to the Lord.

James begins on the foundation of endurance and wisdom, for with these tools, Christians are equipped to persevere. For example, James encourages his audience to view their trials instead as tests, for through these tests, their faith emerges stronger than before. We can endure through suffering because by doing so, we are following in our Savior's footsteps. He chose the cross because He knew the good to come—His people would be secured into the family of God. So, too, we can endure, knowing that one day, we will have peace in the presence of Jesus. The sufferer will receive a "crown of life" for their steadfastness (James 1:12). This "crown" is not the jeweled decoration of royalty, but instead, it is like the laurel wreath that dons the head of a runner at the end of a race—the reward for their endurance. Our strivings are seen and rewarded by our loving Father.

Throughout this chapter, James also corrects potential misconceptions about God. He is not the author of temptations but our sustainer through such temptations. James reminds us that it is our own sinful nature that plants, nurtures, and grows wickedness within us. God is the giver of good gifts. Through the grace offered to us through Jesus's death and resurrection, we can receive wisdom from God to endure trials and uproot sin.

Wisdom is not found in self-help books or the latest podcast. It is found in God and His Word. Throughout the rest of James's letter, he will practically teach his audience how to live in light of God's wisdom, for it is available for anyone who asks and believes. The gospel has the power to change everything—every relationship, every vocation, and every mundane task. How does the gospel change lives? Our job is to ask the Holy Spirit to take God's Word from our heads and plant it into our hearts so that we may carry out His work with our hands.

Questions

READ JAMES 5:19–20, THE LAST TWO VERSES OF JAMES. HOW DO THESE VERSES AND YOUR KNOWLEDGE OF JAMES'S FORMER SKEPTICISM HELP YOU UNDERSTAND JAMES'S GOAL IN WRITING THIS LETTER?

HOW DOES IT CHANGE YOUR UNDERSTANDING OF THIS PASSAGE TO KNOW THAT THE "CROWN OF LIFE" IS NOT A ROYAL CROWN BUT INSTEAD A LAUREL WREATH RESERVED FOR RUNNERS WHO COMPLETE A RACE? *Read 1 Corinthians 9:24–27, which references the same type of crown. What do these verses teach you about endurance?*

AS WE DIVE INTO JAMES, ARGUABLY THE MOST PRACTICAL BOOK IN THE NEW TESTAMENT, TAKE A MOMENT TO EVALUATE YOUR CURRENT RHYTHMS OF LIFE. HOW DO YOU PRACTICALLY HONOR GOD THROUGHOUT YOUR DAYS? *What struggles do you have? How would you like to improve?*

WEEK 44 / DAY 4

James 2 *Practice this week's memory verse.*

ONCE IMPACTED BY THE GOSPEL,
THE LIFE OF A BELIEVER IS NEVER THE SAME.

The Holy Spirit transforms everyday conversations into opportunities to magnify the Lord. Simple household chores become opportunities to serve without complaint. Our motivations become less self-seeking and more Christ-centered. We find a truth that is not dependent on our ever-changing emotions but is fixed on the truth that never changes—Jesus.

This is the foundation of James 2. The gospel empowers us to live differently. Therefore, Christians do not judge like people of the world. Christ judges the heart, not the external appearance (1 Samuel 16:7, James 2:5), and we are called to do the same. When we elevate the rich over the poor, we are misrepresenting the hierarchy of God's kingdom. In fact, in the Beatitudes, Jesus describes His kingdom as poor in spirit, humble, and merciful, not superfluous and affluent (Matthew 5:3–10). Christ does not condemn the poor but instead invites them to be heirs in eternity. Therefore, the Holy Spirit empowers us to love others as we love ourselves, valuing both the rich and the poor as equal image-bearers of God (James 2:8).

The gospel does not only impact the way we see others but also the way we serve. James continues chapter 2 with the harrowing reminder that faith without works is dead; in fact, James repeats this idea twice for emphasis (James 2:17, 2:26). James is not saying that our salvation is secured by our works (Ephesians 2:8–9). Instead, James is describing the transformation that takes place inside the heart of a believer. The Holy Spirit works in our hearts to produce the fruit of the Spirit: love, joy, peace, patience, kindness, goodness, faithfulness, gentleness, and self-control (Galatians 5:22–23). The Holy Spirit is living and active in our hearts, leaving us not as we once were but changing our hearts, our motivations, our words, and our actions to honor Christ and His sacrifice. Others will observe and learn about our faith by our works.

This chapter requires all of us to take a step back and take an inventory of our walk with Christ. Are you quick to judge others? Do you consider the wealthy better than the poor? Are you displaying your faith by serving your loved ones and your community? James 2 reminds us that all of us fall short of the glory of God. Yet, by His grace, He gives mercy. And mercy triumphs over judgment (James 2:13).

Questions

HOW HAS THE GOSPEL CHANGED YOUR LIFE SINCE YOU HAVE ACCEPTED CHRIST AS YOUR LORD AND SAVIOR? *If you have not yet accepted Christ, what change would you like God to make in your life?*

READ MATTHEW 5:3–10. HOW DOES JESUS DESCRIBE HIS KINGDOM? HOW DO JESUS'S WORDS COMPLEMENT JAMES'S WARNING AGAINST FAVORITISM IN JAMES 2:1–12?

WHAT DOES THE PHRASE "FAITH WITHOUT WORKS IS DEAD" MEAN TO YOU? HOW MIGHT YOU "AWAKEN" YOUR FAITH TO ACTION? *Pray for the Holy Spirit to open your eyes to small steps of faith you can take this week.*

WEEK 44 / DAY 5

James 3 *Practice this week's memory verse.*

A METAPHOR IS A LITERARY DEVICE IN WHICH AN AUTHOR COMPARES TWO SEEMINGLY UNRELATED OBJECTS IN ORDER TO EMPHASIZE A SIMILARITY BETWEEN THE TWO.

In James 3, James layers metaphor after metaphor to help paint a picture of the pervasive power of the tongue. The tongue is like a bit in a horse's mouth that controls its direction (James 3:3). It is like a small fire that sets ablaze a large forest (James 3:5) or a ship's rudder that determines its final destination (James 3:4). All of these metaphors communicate one critical truth: the tongue is small but mighty.

In James 4:1, we will see that James addresses the tongue because of dissension that is fracturing the unity of the Jewish churches. Likely, teachers and members within the church body were slandering one another and making decisions with selfish intent (James 3:10, James 3:14). In James 3:9–10, James writes, "With the tongue we bless our Lord and Father, and with it we curse people who are made in God's likeness. Blessing and cursing come out of the same mouth." The tongue acts as a litmus test of character, for the mouth speaks from the heart (Matthew 12:34).

So how do we control the relentless fire that is our tongue? James recommends praying for the wisdom to exercise gentleness in speech. This wisdom does not come from strivings here on earth but is instead from above. God's wisdom is not slanderous or envious or self-seeking. It is peace-loving, gentle, and full of mercy (James 3:17). Only by the Holy Spirit, the presence of God in our lives, are we able to tame the untamable. The gospel changes everything, including the motivations of our hearts and the words that flow forth from it.

If our words are speaking division, we are unable to be cultivators of peace as we are called to be. James invites us to hold up a mirror to ourselves and take a good look at our reflection. Do your words reflect the gospel you believe in? Likely, you have work to do. James describes the tongue as a fire for a reason—it is hard to control. But we are not alone. By God's grace, we can receive the wisdom we need to steward our words with grace.

By God's grace, we can receive the wisdom we need to steward our words with grace.

Questions

TAKE A MOMENT TO OBSERVE ALL THE WAYS THAT JAMES DESCRIBES THE TONGUE IN THIS CHAPTER. WRITE DOWN ALL OF THE METAPHORICAL EXAMPLES. *What do these descriptions communicate about the power of the tongue?*

READ JOHN 14:26, JOHN 16:8, AND JOHN 16:13–15. THESE ARE ALL VERSES ABOUT THE ROLES OF THE HOLY SPIRIT. ALSO READ 2 TIMOTHY 3:16, WHICH IS ABOUT GOD'S WORD. *How do the Holy Spirit and God's Word help us to tame our tongues?*

WEEK 44 / DAY 5

End-of-Week Reflection

Think back on all of the Scripture that you read and studied this week as you answer the questions below.

WHAT DID YOU OBSERVE ABOUT GOD AND HIS CHARACTER?

WHAT DID YOU LEARN ABOUT THE CONDITION OF MANKIND AND YOURSELF?

HOW DOES THIS WEEK'S SCRIPTURE POINT TO THE GOSPEL?

HOW DO THE TRUTHS YOU HAVE LEARNED THIS WEEK ABOUT GOD, MAN, AND THE GOSPEL GIVE YOU HOPE, PEACE, OR ENCOURAGEMENT?

HOW SHOULD YOU RESPOND TO WHAT YOU READ AND LEARNED THIS WEEK?
Write down one or two specific action steps you can take this week to apply what you learned. Then, write a prayer in response to your study of God's Word.

Week Forty-Four Application

Before we begin a new week of study, take some time to apply and share the truths of Scripture you learned this week. Here are a few ideas of how you could do this:

- Schedule a meet-up with a friend to share what you are learning from God's Word.
- Use these prompts to journal or pray through what God is revealing to you through your study of His Word.

— LORD, I FEEL…

— LORD, YOU ARE…

— LORD, FORGIVE ME FOR…

— LORD, HELP ME WITH…

- Spend time worshiping God in a way that is meaningful to you, whether that is taking a walk in nature, painting, drawing, singing, etc.

- Paraphrase the Scripture you read this week.

_____
_____
_____
_____
_____
_____
_____
_____
_____
_____
_____
_____
_____

- Use a study Bible or commentary to help you answer questions that came up as you read this week's Scripture.

- Take steps to fulfill the action steps you listed on Day 5.

- Use highlighters to mark the places you see the metanarrative of Scripture in one or more of the passages that you read this week. (See *The Metanarrative of Scripture* on page 14.)

Week Forty-Five Memory Verse

Therefore, with your minds ready for action, be sober-minded and set your hope completely on the grace to be brought to you at the revelation of Jesus Christ.

1 PETER 1:13

WEEK 45 / DAY 1

James 4
Practice this week's memory verse.

THE FRIEND OF THE WORLD BECOMES THE ENEMY OF GOD (JAMES 4:4).

This verse describes the entirety of James 4, as James exhorts Christians to serve God and God alone. In this chapter, we get a better look at the reason James writes his letter: these churches are attempting to place both God and the world on the throne of their hearts. Their motivations for prayer are self-seeking. They covet one another's circumstances. They treat God like a vending machine—only putting in effort for the blessings they may receive. In Jesus's famous Sermon on The Mount, He teaches, "No one can serve two masters, since either he will hate one and love the other, or he will be devoted to one and despise the other" (Matthew 6:24). This divided worship is no worship at all.

But there is hope. Even when we fail, God gives more grace (James 4:6). James calls his audience to genuine repentance, or the turning away from the grip of sin and falling into the arms of Jesus. James calls them to humility. Double-mindedness reveals a lie that is wedged deep into our souls: the belief that Christ is not enough. In order to genuinely repent before God, we must acknowledge our desperate need for Him. We must submit ourselves to His authority and reclaim what is true: that Christ is all we need. If we draw near to Him, He will be faithful to draw near to us (James 4:8). It is here, in the presence of God, where the weapons that wage war against our souls are ceased. It is here where we finally find peace. In our humbling, we are exalted (James 4:10).

Being humble before God also requires remaining open-handed with our futures. Through the Holy Spirit's faithfulness to sanctify us, our will is gradually conformed to God's will. Instead of clinging to control of our weeks, months, and years, James teaches us how to pray with our hearts and minds open to God's sovereignty: "If the Lord wills, we will live and do this or that" (James 4:15). While even the events of tomorrow are a mystery, we can trust that our coming days are in the hands of the God who has sustained us from the beginning of time. God cares for the birds of the sky and the flowers of the field; surely He will care for us too.

In order to genuinely repent before God, we must acknowledge our desperate need for Him.

Questions

CONSIDER JAMES 4:4. IN WHAT AREAS OF YOUR LIFE
ARE YOU TEMPTED TO BEFRIEND THE WORLD?

READ JAMES 4:7–10 ONCE AGAIN. TAKE NOTE OF THE VERBS
(WORDS USED TO DESCRIBE ACTION) USED IN THESE VERSES.
What do these verbs teach you about repentance and submission to God?

DO YOU STRUGGLE TO TRUST GOD WITH YOUR FUTURE?
HOW DOES THIS PASSAGE TEACH YOU TO COME BEFORE
GOD WITH YOUR ANXIETIES ABOUT TOMORROW?

WEEK 45 / DAY 2

James 5
Practice this week's memory verse.

JAMES CLOSES HIS LETTER IN CHAPTER 5 WITH ADMONITIONS FOR THE RICH.

Although wealth is not explicitly condemned in the Bible (Proverbs 10:22), Scripture calls believers to be generous in good deeds and to protect the poor (Proverbs 19:17, 22:9, 22:16). Apparently, some to whom James writes are not using their wealth to protect the vulnerable. Instead, they are living in self-indulgence and not paying for their employees' labor. James condemns this financial abuse and reminds them that God will repay them for every deed. He advises his audience to conduct themselves in light of one central truth: Jesus is coming again. In light of this, Christians are to live holy lives, full of patience and prayer.

First, James encourages believers to be patient as they wait for the Lord's coming. Like farmers who must wait patiently for the harvest, so also believers are called to wait upon the Lord. As James gives this command, he also shares insights on how to wait patiently—that is, by looking to the examples of the prophets. James also encourages his readers to pray in every situation—whether sick or well, happy or sad. As James gives this exhortation, he looks again to the examples of the prophets and mentions Elijah, who prayed that it would not rain for three years and six months (1 Kings 17–18).

James explains that there is great power in a righteous person's prayers (James 5:16). Finally, James concludes his letter by instructing the church to continue to care for one another by praying for one another (James 5:13–18), confessing their sins to one another (James 5:16), and pursuing wandering brothers and sisters (James 5:19–20).

As James repeats, so we, too, believe: Jesus is coming soon. He is the steadfast Judge, who is coming to make all things right (James 5:9). Yet for all who have trusted in Jesus, we need not fear God's wrath on the day of judgment. Because of Jesus's finished work on the cross, we can approach the throne of God with confidence, knowing that we will be forgiven for every sin. God has saved us through the blood of His Son, and in light of Jesus's sacrifice, He calls us to live steadfast and godly lives. Let us live with faith and perseverance as we wait patiently on Him, remembering that God is the just and perfect Judge. He is the compassionate and merciful King, and He is coming again.

Questions

TAKE AN INVENTORY OF YOUR GIVING HABITS (JAMES 5:1–6). WHAT DOES YOUR FINANCIAL SPENDING REVEAL ABOUT YOUR PRIORITIES?

JAMES ENCOURAGES HIS READERS TO REMEMBER THE EXAMPLES OF FAITHFUL WITNESSES IN THE PAST. SPEND TIME REFLECTING ON THE LIVES OF FAITHFUL BELIEVERS YOU KNOW. *If they are still alive, let them know how their example has encouraged your faith.*

SPEND AN EXTENDED AMOUNT OF TIME IN PRAYER (JAMES 5:13–18). EXPRESS YOUR PRAISE TO THE LORD, AS WELL AS ANY CONCERNS THAT YOU HAVE ON YOUR HEART. WRITE YOUR PRAYER BELOW.

THE BOOK OF
1 Peter

DATE WRITTEN	c. AD 64–65
AUTHOR	This book was written by the Apostle Peter, a beloved disciple of Jesus Christ.
AUDIENCE	The book of 1 Peter is addressed to Christians dispersed throughout Asia Minor, most likely Gentile believers who were displaced and exiled due to persecution. In this letter, Peter emphasizes perseverance through suffering for God's chosen people.
HISTORICAL CONTEXT	Many scholars believe that Peter's audience was experiencing discrimination and persecution for their beliefs from local Roman authorities. Christianity posed a threat to the Roman Empire that cherished their freedom to do and live however they pleased. Peter encourages these believers to endure just as Christ did and to live honorable lives that point to the gospel, despite persecution.
GENRE	*Epistle*
KEY WORDS	*Inheritance, Suffering, Glory*
THEMES	1. Christians can persevere through suffering, knowing there is an imperishable inheritance awaiting them in heaven. 2. Those who place their faith in Jesus receive new life, and this new life propels us to live in holiness.
KEY VERSE	*You rejoice in this, even though now for a short time, if necessary, you suffer grief in various trials so that the proven character of your faith—more valuable than gold which, though perishable, is refined by fire—may result in praise, glory, and honor at the revelation of Jesus Christ.* —1 Peter 1:6–7

WEEK 45 / DAY 3

1 Peter 1 *Practice this week's memory verse.*

HOW DO WE LIVE IN A WORLD THAT IS NOT OUR HOME AS BELIEVERS?
HOW ARE WE TO REMAIN HOPEFUL AND STEADFAST DURING SUFFERING?

These are the questions Peter addresses in his letter. From the beginning of the letter, we learn Peter is writing to those he calls "exiles dispersed abroad" (1 Peter 1:1). While Peter is writing to Jewish Christians who lived in specific places in Asia Minor—which is located in modern-day Turkey—the phrase "exiles dispersed abroad" also applies to us as modern-day readers. As followers of Christ, our true home is with God in heaven. Therefore, we spiritually live as exiles in a broken world. As we await the day that we are home with Christ, Peter's words encourage us to live as exiles with joy and endurance.

Joy and endurance are rooted in the living hope we have in Christ. In 1 Peter 1:3–5, Peter describes how in His great mercy, God has birthed us into a living hope through the death and resurrection of Christ. He has given us an inheritance that can never be tainted or taken away. And this inheritance is kept in heaven for us. As we wait to one day receive this inheritance, we are being guarded by God's power. God is holding us in His hands, promising to keep us secure before we are rescued from this world of darkness and brought into His eternal glory.

This hope causes these believers, and us as well, to rejoice even in suffering. Paul reminds believers of the purpose of our suffering in 1 Peter 1:6–9. The trials we suffer as believers sanctify us and strengthen our faith. Our faith in Christ, even in times of trouble, gives God glory and transforms us more into the image of Christ. As we undergo trials, we rejoice as we consider our living hope in heaven. But we also rejoice as we consider the Savior we love. Although we cannot see Christ, we love Him and believe in Him. Our belief in Christ and our love for Christ cause us to rejoice, not only because of what He has done for us but also because of what He will one day do for us. In times of suffering, we look forward to the day when Christ will take us from this broken world, make us new, and live with us for all eternity.

As we undergo trials, we rejoice as we consider our living hope in heaven.

Questions

HOW DOES KNOWING YOU HAVE A LIVING HOPE IN CHRIST ENCOURAGE YOU IN THE PRESENT?

HOW DOES PETER DRAW COMPARISONS BETWEEN WHAT IS PERISHABLE AND IMPERISHABLE IN THIS CHAPTER?

WHAT DOES PETER TEACH ABOUT GOD'S WORD IN 1 PETER 1:23–25? WHY IS THIS IMPORTANT?

WEEK 45 / DAY 4

1 Peter 2 *Practice this week's memory verse.*

PETER CONTINUES TO ENCOURAGE BELIEVERS AS THEY LIVE IN A BROKEN WORLD.

In chapter 1, Peter exhorted Christians to live holy lives as they await the day they are with Christ. We see this theme continued in this chapter, reminding us that how we live in the present matters as believers. Christ has saved us and given us new life in Him. Therefore, we are to walk as the holy people God has created us and called us to be.

Peter describes this holy living with imagery that would be familiar to Jewish Christians. He writes in verses 5 that believers are "living stones, a spiritual house . . . being built to be a holy priesthood to offer spiritual sacrifices acceptable to God through Jesus Christ." With this language, Peter points to the tabernacle and the temple, where priests would offer sacrifices to God. Like the priests of old, believers are being formed into holy people, tasked to give sacrifices to God through Christ. First Corinthians 6:19 takes this idea a step further, describing our bodies as God's new spiritual temple. By comparing the believer's identity in Christ to the temple and the priests, Peter helps us see how we are to be holy people who spiritually give God sacrifices through our obedience to Him.

In 1 Peter 2:6–10, Peter reminds us how Jesus is the cornerstone upon which the body of Christ is built. He quotes Isaiah 28:16, Psalm 118:22, and Isaiah 8:14, which all point to Jesus. During His time on earth, Jesus was rejected by many. But even though Christ was rejected and eventually killed, He was victorious. He conquered sin and death on the cross and rose from the grave, uniting all believers in Him. Those who trust in Jesus are considered a chosen race, a royal priesthood, a holy nation, and a people for God's possession (1 Peter 2:9).

This imagery is also something Jewish Christians would be familiar with. The nation of Israel was God's chosen and set-apart people. But now, all those who believe in Christ are God's chosen and set-apart people. As God's people, we are to tell the world of the God who has brought us out of darkness and into His light. While we share God's mercy and love, we are to walk in holiness. Peter urges these believers, and us, to abstain from sin and live honorably among people who oppose God. As we remain obedient to God, we will demonstrate to the world the goodness and grace of our great God.

Questions

HOW DOES GOD'S WORD MATURE US AS BELIEVERS?

HOW DOES OUR POSITION IN CHRIST THAT PETER DECLARES IN
1 PETER 2:9–10 IMPACT THE WAY WE LIVE AS BELIEVERS?

ACCORDING TO 1 PETER 2:21–25, HOW DO CHRIST'S ACTIONS
IN SUFFERING IMPACT OUR OWN AS BELIEVERS?

WEEK 45 / DAY 5

1 Peter 3 *Practice this week's memory verse.*

AT THE END OF 1 PETER 2, PETER GAVE INSTRUCTION AND ENCOURAGEMENT TO SLAVES IN THE FIRST CENTURY, TEACHING WHAT IT LOOKS LIKE TO SUBMIT TO THEIR MASTERS, OR OBEY WITH HUMILITY.

Now, in 1 Peter 3, he gives wives instructions on what it looks like to submit to their husbands. Although Peter begins by addressing wives in this chapter, Peter also addresses all believers. He teaches how wives are called to submit to their husbands, but all believers are to ultimately submit to God, especially when they experience suffering.

As previously mentioned, Peter first instructs wives to submit to their husbands. Biblical submission involves wives humbly yielding to the leadership of their husbands as their husbands seek to follow the Lord and lead their families in the Lord. And Peter reveals how submission can encourage husbands in their own behavior. As wives live pure and reverent lives, exemplified in many ways but specifically through submission, husbands can be encouraged to live purely and reverently as well. In verse 7, Peter instructs husbands to treat their wives with understanding and respect. Husbands are to view their wives as coheirs of Christ's grace and treat them as such.

Peter then moves on to give general instructions to all believers about their behavior. He instructs believers to be like-minded, sympathetic, compassionate, and humble. In times of reviling or suffering, believers are not to seek vengeance or return insult. Instead, they are to seek peace and keep their mouths pure. Peter goes on to address a believer's behavior during suffering, writing in verses 13–17 that believers should not be afraid or intimidated by those who cause them suffering. When others oppose and question them, believers should remain ready to defend their faith with gentleness and respect.

Peter's words in these verses point back to 1 Peter 2:20–25. As he did in chapter 2, Peter connects the suffering of believers to the suffering of Christ. Just as Christ suffered, so will believers suffer. While suffering is difficult, believers have the hope of salvation in their suffering. Just as God brought Noah and his family out of the waters of judgment (Genesis 6–8), so has God brought believers out of the waters of judgment through Christ. Therefore, believers have confidence that God will deliver them from suffering just as He has delivered them from sin and death.

Questions

ACCORDING TO VERSES 10–12, HOW DOES GOD'S RELATIONSHIP
WITH US AS BELIEVERS IMPACT OUR OBEDIENCE?

WHY IS IT IMPORTANT THAT WE DEFEND OUR FAITH
WITH GENTLENESS AND REVERENCE?

WEEK 45 / DAY 5

End-of-Week Reflection

Think back on all of the Scripture that you read and studied this week as you answer the questions below.

WHAT DID YOU OBSERVE ABOUT GOD AND HIS CHARACTER?

WHAT DID YOU LEARN ABOUT THE CONDITION OF MANKIND AND YOURSELF?

HOW DOES THIS WEEK'S SCRIPTURE POINT TO THE GOSPEL?

HOW DO THE TRUTHS YOU HAVE LEARNED THIS WEEK ABOUT GOD, MAN, AND THE GOSPEL GIVE YOU HOPE, PEACE, OR ENCOURAGEMENT?

HOW SHOULD YOU RESPOND TO WHAT YOU READ AND LEARNED THIS WEEK?
Write down one or two specific action steps you can take this week to apply what you learned. Then, write a prayer in response to your study of God's Word.

Week Forty-Five Application

Before we begin a new week of study, take some time to apply and share the truths of Scripture you learned this week. Here are a few ideas of how you could do this:

- Schedule a meet-up with a friend to share what you are learning from God's Word.
- Use these prompts to journal or pray through what God is revealing to you through your study of His Word.

— LORD, I FEEL...

— LORD, YOU ARE...

— LORD, FORGIVE ME FOR...

— LORD, HELP ME WITH...

- Spend time worshiping God in a way that is meaningful to you, whether that is taking a walk in nature, painting, drawing, singing, etc.

- Paraphrase the Scripture you read this week.

_____
_____
_____
_____
_____
_____
_____
_____
_____
_____
_____
_____
_____
_____
_____

- Use a study Bible or commentary to help you answer questions that came up as you read this week's Scripture.

- Take steps to fulfill the action steps you listed on Day 5.

- Use highlighters to mark the places you see the metanarrative of Scripture in one or more of the passages that you read this week. (See *The Metanarrative of Scripture* on page 14.)

Week Forty-Six Memory Verse

Above all, maintain constant love for one another, since love covers a multitude of sins.

1 PETER 4:8

WEEK 46 / DAY 1

1 Peter 4 *Practice this week's memory verse.*

IN HIS LETTER SO FAR, PETER HAS ADDRESSED THE TOPIC OF SUFFERING AND HOW CHRISTIANS ARE TO EMBRACE SUFFERING IN A BROKEN WORLD.

Peter continues to speak about suffering in chapter 4, giving believers more instruction and encouragement as they live among those who oppose God and His ways.

In verse 1, Peter connects Christ's suffering with the believer's suffering once again. But this time, he does so to make a point about sin. Those who are in Christ are finished with sin. This does not mean that believers cannot sin but that believers no longer pursue and delight in sin. Jesus suffered and died on the cross to free believers from sin. Believers live in light of their freedom from sin by doing what is right and opposing sin, even if they suffer for doing so.

Peter then writes in verses 2–3 how believers live for God's will rather than their human desires. This is surprising to those in the world who do not know Jesus Christ. Unbelievers live for their own desires, and they are often taken aback by believers who do not join them in their sinful ways. Sadly, unbelievers will have to stand before God's throne one day and be judged for their wickedness. But those who believe in the gospel will be saved from their sin and granted eternal life in Christ (1 Peter 4:6).

As believers await the day when Christ returns to set things right, they are to live intentionally in the present. Peter encourages believers to be alert and sober-minded, specifically in prayer. He reminds them of the importance of loving others and being hospitable people. In verses 10–11, Peter exhorts believers to exercise the spiritual gifts God has given them. Doing so will strengthen the body of Christ and glorify the Lord.

Peter concludes this chapter by returning to the theme of suffering. In verses 12–13, Peter encourages believers not to be surprised by suffering. Suffering will happen to believers, but as believers, we can rejoice in our sufferings. Why? Because we share in the sufferings of Christ. Believers suffer for the sake of Christ and identify with His suffering on the cross in their affliction. Paul reminds believers once again that it is better to suffer for doing good than evil (1 Peter 4:14–19). Although suffering is difficult, we can entrust ourselves to the Lord in our suffering and continue to pursue obedience to Him.

Questions

WHAT DOES IT LOOK LIKE TO LIVE FOR GOD'S WILL OVER HUMAN DESIRES?

HOW DOES 1 PETER 4:12–19 GIVE YOU HOPE AND COMFORT IN SUFFERING?

WHAT DOES IT LOOK LIKE TO PRACTICALLY ENTRUST YOURSELF TO GOD DURING SUFFERING?

WEEK 46 / DAY 2

1 Peter 5 *Practice this week's memory verse.*

IN TODAY'S READING, WE COME TO THE END OF 1 PETER. THE MESSAGE OF 1 PETER IS ONE OF ENCOURAGEMENT AND ENDURANCE IN THE FACE OF PERSECUTION AND SUFFERING.

Throughout the book, Peter reminds the Jewish Christians living abroad in Asia Minor that believers are a chosen people called to live for Christ in all they do. And here in chapter 5, Peter provides final exhortations to these believers as they await the return of Jesus Christ.

In verses 1–4, Peter addresses the elders who lead their churches. As a fellow elder, Peter calls these men throughout Asia Minor to shepherd God's flock well. They are to lead joyfully and not out of a sense of obligation. And they are called to be examples to their flocks and not function out of greed or a prideful lordship over the people. They are to do this out of love for the true Shepherd, who will one day return for them. Peter then encourages those who are younger to follow the leadership of the elders that God has placed over them. But then, in verse 5, Peter reminds both the elders and those who serve under them to show humility toward each other.

Humility serves as the driving force for Peter's final encouragement to these churches. He quotes a familiar verse from Proverbs 3:34 to support his point that grace is given to the humble, not the proud. Humility breeds a heart that is willing to place all our worries at the feet of Jesus because He is the ultimate example of humility. He can bear all of our burdens because He bore all our sin on the cross. We now stand firm in our faith against the adversary because of Christ's victory over Satan. And we stand firm because we also have the support and encouragement of our fellow believers around the world.

Peter ends this letter by reminding us that Jesus will return for us one day. When He does, we will experience complete restoration. He will establish and strengthen us, and we will worship Him forever. Though our suffering on this earth may be for a short time, we can trust His support, care, and love until He comes. As we wait, we stand firm in the grace of God.

Humility breeds a heart that is willing to place all our worries at the feet of Jesus.

Questions

WHY IS HUMILITY WITHIN THE CHURCH IMPORTANT? WHY SHOULD ELDERS AND GOD'S FLOCK EXHIBIT HUMILITY TOWARD EACH OTHER?

IN 1 PETER 5:8, PETER TELLS BELIEVERS TO BE SOBER-MINDED AND ALERT AGAINST THE ADVERSARY AS WE AWAIT CHRIST'S RETURN. WHAT DOES THIS MEAN? *Read Philippians 1:27, 1 Corinthians 16:13, and Ephesians 6:18 to help you answer.*

WHEN YOU FACE HOSTILITY FOR YOUR FAITH, HOW DOES THE MESSAGE OF 1 PETER ENCOURAGE YOU TO STAND FIRM AND ENDURE SUFFERING?

The knowledge of Jesus Christ compels believers to live a life of godliness.

THE BOOK OF 2 Peter

DATE WRITTEN	c. AD 65–68
AUTHOR	This book was also written by Peter, the apostle and disciple of Jesus.
AUDIENCE	The audience of 2 Peter is believed to be the same as 1 Peter—churches dispersed throughout Asia Minor. Peter likely penned this letter shortly before his martyrdom in Rome. Knowing his death was imminent, Peter used this letter to share his final exhortation for the churches in Asia Minor. Peter sought to encourage them to stand firm in their faith, forsaking false teachings and impurity.
HISTORICAL CONTEXT	Peter's two letters traveled throughout the Roman-occupied region of Asia Minor to encourage believers from church to church. Persecution from Roman authorities was common. Peter, guided by the Holy Spirit, wrote to strengthen their faith and remind them of the hope they have in Christ and His return.
GENRE	*Epistle*
KEY WORDS	*Knowledge, Endurance, Suffering*
THEMES	1. Christians are to stand firm in the truth of God's Word in face of trials and opposition, for it is trustworthy. 2. The knowledge of Jesus Christ is the lens through which believers see the world. This knowledge empowers believers to flee from sin and pursue righteousness.
KEY VERSE	*His divine power has given us everything required for life and godliness through the knowledge of him who called us by his own glory and goodness.* —2 Peter 1:3

WEEK 46 / DAY 3

2 Peter 1
Practice this week's memory verse.

TODAY, WE BEGIN THE BOOK OF 2 PETER.

In this letter, Peter addresses the same audience from his first letter—the Jewish Christians living as exiles in Asia Minor, which is located in modern-day Turkey. Peter, likely imprisoned in Rome as he writes, knows his own time on the earth is short due to the increased persecution of Christians. In this letter, he reminds believers of the truth of the gospel. And in chapter 1 specifically, he reminds them that the knowledge of Jesus Christ compels believers to live a life of godliness.

Peter begins by stating who Jesus is and what He has done for us. It is through His divine power, His great and precious promises, and His divine nature that we are able to escape the corruption of our world. As a result, we take great pains to enrich our faith through goodness, knowledge, self-control, endurance, and godliness. Each of these builds upon one another to enable believers to remain useful and faithful as we await Christ's return. Peter also provides a warning. If we lack these things, we are blind and short-sighted, and we forget the great price Jesus paid for our sins. We must remember that we are called, and Jesus has provided an eternal home for us.

Peter tells his readers that even though they may know these truths, he will never stop reminding them. Peter himself needed continual reminders of who Jesus was, even after being in His presence each day. His eyewitness account, specifically on the Mount of Transfiguration, proclaims that Jesus is the Son of God (Matthew 17:1–13, Mark 9:2–13, Luke 9:28–36). But Peter also reminds us that all of Scripture, though written by men, never came from their own thought or interpretation but through the leading of the Holy Spirit. We can trust the Bible because God is the author, and He alone weaves the thread of redemption through every page.

This short chapter in 2 Peter provides us with several reminders and imperatives. Perhaps one of the most practical steps believers can take is found in verse 19. Peter tells us to pay attention to the prophetic Word because it is the lamp shining in the darkness. The Bible is the tool that provides us with knowledge of our Savior. When our hearts are focused on Jesus, we grow in godliness as we wait for Him, our Morning Star, to return.

Questions

HOW CAN YOU PRACTICALLY EXHIBIT EACH OF THE CHARACTERISTICS BELOW TO ENRICH YOUR FAITH?

Goodness

Knowledge

Self-Control

Endurance

Godliness

WHY DO BELIEVERS NEED A CONSTANT REMINDER OF THE TRUTHS OF THE GOSPEL?

HOW DOES 2 PETER 1:20 REMIND BELIEVERS THAT THE BIBLE IS THE VERY WORD OF GOD? WHY CAN YOU TRUST SCRIPTURE TO GUIDE YOU IN LIFE?

WEEK 46 / DAY 4

2 Peter 2 *Practice this week's memory verse.*

HAVE YOU EVER EXPERIENCED THE PERFECT STORM OF TRIALS ALL AT ONCE? SUDDENLY, WITHOUT WARNING, EVERYTHING SEEMS TO GO SIDEWAYS.

This is the reality for Peter's audience—the churches in Asia Minor. Scholars believe that these churches were experiencing persecution from the Roman Empire at this time. To make matters worse, false teachers were perverting the truth of the gospel. Although it is impossible to know what exactly these false teachers were promoting, we do know that their teachings, combined with the persecution these churches faced, led to many Christians straying away from the truth (2 Peter 2:2). In 2 Peter 2, Peter speaks vehemently against these false teachers and reminds the churches of God's perfect justice.

In fact, Peter repeats the word "destroyed" or "destruction" six times throughout this chapter in order to emphasize the point that false teachers who attempt to destroy Christ's Church will one day meet the final destruction of God. Throughout the Bible, we learn about God's patience with sinners, but we also learn about His wrath toward stubborn disobedience. Peter highlights many Old Testament examples of God's wrath against sin. God sent a flood upon the world but saved Noah (Genesis 6–8). He reduced the cities of Sodom and Gomorrah to ashes but saved Abraham's cousin Lot (Genesis 19:1–29). Peter reminds us that God has complete knowledge and complete control of evil in the world. In His sovereignty, God will eventually rescue the faithful and oust the evil from His creation.

This is the impending fate of the false teachers, for their empty promises malign the way of truth (2 Peter 2:2). Peter informs us that these teachers have an understanding of Jesus Christ but choose to pervert the gospel for their own gain (2 Peter 2:3, 2:20). Their arrogance and bold disregard for truth only leads to ruin, for Scripture calls them "springs without water" (2 Peter 2:17). Peter's descriptions of these false teachers serve as both a warning and a comfort for God's people. This message warns us of falling prey to harmful distortions of the gospel; it also comforts us, for we know that justice lies only in God's hands. One day, our heavenly Father will right every wrong. Those who love Him are secure under His wings. For the faithful, He is a shield (Psalm 91:4).

Questions

UNDERLINE OR HIGHLIGHT IN YOUR BIBLE THE MENTIONS OF "DESTROYED," OR "DESTRUCTION" IN THIS PASSAGE. WHY DO YOU THINK THAT PETER USED THESE WORDS IN PARTICULAR?

AT THE END OF THE CHAPTER, PETER QUOTES A PROVERB FROM PROVERBS 26. READ PROVERBS 26. WHAT DOES THE PROVERB'S TEACHING ABOUT "FOOLS" TEACH YOU ABOUT FALSE TEACHERS?

LIKE PETER'S AUDIENCE, WE, TOO, CAN BE SWAYED BY LIES THAT OUR CULTURE TELLS US. WHAT LIES OF CULTURE MIGHT YOU BE BELIEVING TODAY? WHAT DOES GOD'S WORD HAVE TO SAY ABOUT THESE LIES?
(For example: more money leads to more happiness, individuals define their own truth, career success will make us feel fulfilled, etc.)

WEEK 46 / DAY 5

2 Peter 3 *Practice this week's memory verse.*

LET US REMEMBER PETER'S CONTEXT WHILE WRITING THE BOOK OF 2 PETER.

Scholars believe that Peter is likely imprisoned in Rome, staring down his impending death. As church tradition details, he will soon be crucified upside down, for he did not want to die upright like his Savior. Peter is keenly aware that the end is near. With this perspective, he brings his second letter to a close.

Peter leaves a profound legacy for how Christians should disciple one another: by remembering God's Word. By His words, God created the heavens and the earth. And by His word and in His timing, the earth we know will pass away, and His glorious kingdom will burst forth. The false teachers gravely underestimate the power of God's Word. But we know the truth. Their ministry is temporary, but God's is eternal. This should serve as a comfort for the Church, for there is no threat and no false teacher that can "separate us from the love of God" (Romans 8:39).

However, in the meantime, Peter warns that false teachers will attempt to cause destruction while they are able. In fact, in order to diminish God's authority, the false teachers were spreading rumors that God was delaying His second coming. Yet God is not delaying, but He is extending patience to humanity by allowing sinners the proper time to return and repent (2 Peter 3:9). The waiting we experience now is not by accident. God transcends time, and therefore, He controls it. Peter references Psalm 90:4 when he writes, "With the Lord one day is like a thousand years, and a thousand years like one day" (2 Peter 3:8). While we wait in the unknown on this side of heaven, we have the privilege of trusting the one true God, who always comes through on His promises.

With this in mind, Peter encourages his audience to be ready for Jesus's return, or "the day of the Lord." This will not be an expected day; it will "come like a thief" (2 Peter 3:10). Therefore, Christians must be ready. Let the Holy Spirit move us to action while we wait expectantly for Christ's coming kingdom. Stand firm. Cling to the gospel. Rid yourself of unrepentant sin. Give generously to those in need—for soon, the temporary pleasures on earth will fade, and only glory will remain. One day, the evil of the world will be defeated, and we will have peace. Let our legacy, like Peter's, cry out: "To him be the glory both now and to the day of eternity" (2 Peter 3:18).

Questions

TAKE A MOMENT TO SUMMARIZE 2 PETER IN TWO TO THREE SENTENCES IN THE SPACE BELOW.

READ ISAIAH 13:9, JOEL 2:11, AND ZEPHANIAH 1:14. HOW IS THE "DAY OF THE LORD" DESCRIBED IN THESE OLD TESTAMENT PASSAGES? *How does Jesus change the "day of the Lord" for those who trust Him as their Savior?*

WEEK 46 / DAY 5

End-of-Week Reflection

Think back on all of the Scripture that you read and studied this week as you answer the questions below.

WHAT DID YOU OBSERVE ABOUT GOD AND HIS CHARACTER?

WHAT DID YOU LEARN ABOUT THE CONDITION OF MANKIND AND YOURSELF?

HOW DOES THIS WEEK'S SCRIPTURE POINT TO THE GOSPEL?

HOW DO THE TRUTHS YOU HAVE LEARNED THIS WEEK ABOUT GOD, MAN, AND THE GOSPEL GIVE YOU HOPE, PEACE, OR ENCOURAGEMENT?

HOW SHOULD YOU RESPOND TO WHAT YOU READ AND LEARNED THIS WEEK?
Write down one or two specific action steps you can take this week to apply what you learned. Then, write a prayer in response to your study of God's Word.

Week Forty-Six Application

Before we begin a new week of study, take some time to apply and share the truths of Scripture you learned this week. Here are a few ideas of how you could do this:

- Schedule a meet-up with a friend to share what you are learning from God's Word.
- Use these prompts to journal or pray through what God is revealing to you through your study of His Word.

— LORD, I FEEL...

_____

_____

_____

— LORD, YOU ARE...

_____

_____

_____

— LORD, FORGIVE ME FOR...

_____

_____

_____

— LORD, HELP ME WITH...

_____

_____

_____

- Spend time worshiping God in a way that is meaningful to you, whether that is taking a walk in nature, painting, drawing, singing, etc.

- Paraphrase the Scripture you read this week.

_____
_____
_____
_____
_____
_____
_____
_____
_____
_____
_____
_____

- Use a study Bible or commentary to help you answer questions that came up as you read this week's Scripture.

- Take steps to fulfill the action steps you listed on Day 5.

- Use highlighters to mark the places you see the metanarrative of Scripture in one or more of the passages that you read this week. (See *The Metanarrative of Scripture* on page 14.)

Because God is light, His children walk in the light; they no longer walk in the darkness.

THE BOOK OF
1 John

DATE WRITTEN	c. AD 85–95
AUTHOR	John, the son of Zebedee and disciple of Jesus, wrote this letter along with 2 and 3 John, as well as the Gospel of John and Revelation. After Jesus's resurrection, John became a leader in the early church, specifically leading the churches in the city of Ephesus.
AUDIENCE	John wrote to the group of house churches in Ephesus and the surrounding region that he oversaw. These churches experienced strife as groups broke away from the church and denied Jesus as Messiah. John teaches believers that true love for God manifests itself through obedience to His commands and love for their brothers and sisters in Christ.
HISTORICAL CONTEXT	While ministering in Ephesus, John saw a rise in false teaching within the Church. John writes to encourage Christians to affirm proper theology and remember that God sent His Son as the true Light of the World.
GENRE	*Epistle*
KEY WORDS	*Love, Believe, Remain*
THEMES	1. Jesus, the Son of God, is the Light of the World. 2. Christians should grow in faith, obedience, and love through the knowledge of God and the power of the Spirit.
KEY VERSE	*If we walk in the light as he himself is in the light, we have fellowship with one another, and the blood of Jesus his Son cleanses us from all sin.* —1 John 1:7

Week Forty-Seven Memory Verse

If we confess our sins, he is faithful and righteous to forgive us our sins and to cleanse us from all unrighteousness.

1 JOHN 1:9

WEEK 47 / DAY 1

1 John 1 *Practice this week's memory verse.*

IMAGINE THAT YOU ARE A MEMBER OF A CHURCH IN THE CITY OF EPHESUS.

You are among other believers who profess to know God and have a relationship with Him. But some people begin to declare beliefs that do not find their grounding in the gospel. They try to convince you and others of their teaching, and these teachers eventually leave the church because of their views.

Even though you did not buy into their teaching, you feel shaken up in your faith. Doubts and questions fill your mind over the truth of the gospel. This is the situation in which the Apostle John writes this letter, likely while living in Ephesus before being imprisoned on the island of Patmos. In light of false teachers who departed from the church, John exhorts the remaining believers to remain firm in their faith. John primarily does this by assuring the believers of the truth of the gospel and the validity of their salvation.

In verses 1–3, John testifies to the humanity of Jesus. It is likely that the false teachers do not affirm that Jesus, the Son of God and the Christ, took on human flesh. John dispels this belief by declaring how he, and many others, heard Christ's voice, saw Him with their eyes, and felt Him with their hands. This testimony of Christ's humanity is being declared to these believers so that they can have fellowship with John and the other apostles. Because they are believers, this fellowship is something they already have access to enjoy—but John is likely reminding them of this truth so the church can rest in what is true and participate in the body of Christ.

John reveals how believers have fellowship with one another but also with the Father and Christ (1 John 1:3). In the following verses, John teaches how we can know if someone has genuine fellowship with God or not: if someone claims to have a relationship with God but either denies their sinfulness or walks in the darkness of sin, they are not a true believer. Because God is light, His children walk in the light; they no longer walk in the darkness. That said, believers will still struggle against sin. John provides hope for this struggle in verses 7–9. Though our struggle against sin is difficult, we can be comforted by knowing that Christ has forgiven our sin. And we can be comforted when we confess our sins to God, knowing that God is always faithful to forgive us.

Questions

HOW WOULD A PERSONAL TESTIMONY OF CHRIST'S HUMANITY ENCOURAGE THE BELIEVERS JOHN IS WRITING TO? HOW ARE PERSONAL TESTIMONIES IMPACTFUL TO YOU?

HOW DOES OUR FELLOWSHIP WITH GOD INFLUENCE THE WAY WE LIVE AS BELIEVERS?

HOW DOES KNOWING GOD IS FAITHFUL TO FORGIVE ENCOURAGE YOU TO CONFESS YOUR SINS TO GOD?

WEEK 47 / DAY 2

1 John 2 *Practice this week's memory verse.*

IN 1 JOHN 2, JOHN CONTINUES TO WRITE ENCOURAGEMENT TO THE GROUP OF BELIEVERS IN EPHESUS.

In this second chapter, John reminds the church once again in verses 1–2 of the hope they have when they sin. While John exhorts them not to sin, he reminds them how Jesus is an advocate for all believers. When we sin, Jesus declares our freedom from guilt and punishment to God. Jesus is also our atoning sacrifice. On the cross, Jesus sacrificed Himself so that those who believe in Him could be forgiven. Therefore, as believers, we can find hope when we sin by remembering Christ's atoning sacrifice and hoping in Christ's role as our advocate.

As he did in the first chapter, John draws distinctions between those who do know Christ and those who do not. The first distinction involves obedience (1 John 2:3–6). Believers can know with confidence that they belong to the Lord by their obedience to God. However, the person who says they know God but does not consistently obey God is likely not a genuine follower of Christ. As believers, we are to walk as Jesus walked. While we cannot be perfect like Jesus was perfect, we can follow in Christ's footsteps by obeying God's commands with the help of the Holy Spirit.

The second distinction involves love. God commands believers to love one another (Mark 12:31), and those who claim to know God will love others. However, those who consistently hate others are not genuine followers of Christ. As believers, we show that we walk in God's light and love through our love for others. Those whose lives are marked by hatred rather than love reveal that they remain in darkness.

In the last part of 1 John 2, John continues to reveal the characteristics of true believers. In verses 15–17, John teaches that believers do not love the world or the things in this world. John is speaking about the sinful aspects of our world that are against God and His law. Rather than pursuing worldly lusts, believers are to pursue God's will. Verses 18–23 reveal another distinction. Those who do not know Jesus deny that Jesus is the Messiah, the One promised by God to bring about salvation. The people who left the church denied this essential truth, revealing that they were not true believers. However, those who confess that Jesus is the Messiah and the Son of God are true believers. Believers are blessed with a relationship with God and respond to this relationship with works of obedience and love.

Questions

WHY IS IT IMPORTANT FOR BELIEVERS TO BE OBEDIENT?
HOW DOES OBEDIENCE TO GOD REVEAL OUR RELATIONSHIP WITH GOD?

REVIEW JOHN'S REASONS FOR WRITING IN VERSES 12–14.
WHAT REASON STICKS OUT TO YOU THE MOST AND WHY?

IN THIS CHAPTER, JOHN CALLS BELIEVERS TO LOVE OTHERS
(VERSES 9–11), BUT HE ALSO INSTRUCTS THEM NOT TO LOVE THE WORLD
AND ITS SINFULNESS (VERSES 15–17). *What does it look like for you to live in this tension of loving others but not loving the sinful world in which we live?*

WEEK 47 / DAY 3

1 John 3 *Practice this week's memory verse.*

JOHN HAS ALREADY MADE IT CLEAR THAT TRUE BELIEVERS LOVE OTHERS, AND IN 1 JOHN 3, JOHN CONTINUES TO EMPHASIZE THIS TRUTH.

John deepens the topic of love in this chapter, revealing how we come to know love as believers and what it looks like to live in light of that love. Before speaking about believers' love, John talks about God's love. He writes in verse 1 that God's great love is declared to believers through Him calling them His children. Those who come to faith in Christ are brought into God's family and declared children of God. God did not have to bring us into His family, but His decision to do so through Jesus displays His great love.

As God's children, we receive numerous blessings. One of these blessings is that we will one day be free of sin and transformed to be like Christ. John speaks of this truth in verses 2–3. One day, all believers will see Christ face to face and be made like Him, perfectly pure. But until that day, we are to purify ourselves in the present by putting off sin and walking in righteousness. John writes in verses 4–10 that God's children do not pursue sinful living. Because Jesus has made us righteous, or positionally holy, we walk in righteousness by doing what is right and honoring to the Lord. A pattern of consistent sin, or unrighteousness, does not reveal a heart that Christ has transformed. In contrast, true believers will display a life marked by righteous living because they have been given the righteousness of Christ.

The remainder of 1 John focuses on the love believers should demonstrate. Rather than hating others, we are to love them. As believers, our ability to know and show love is given through Jesus Christ. Love is demonstrated by Jesus, who laid down His life for us. In response, believers are to lay down their own lives for others through their sacrificial love. If Jesus sacrificed Himself for us, so are we to sacrifice ourselves for others. Doing so will demonstrate to others the amazing love of Christ. And even if we fail to love others as we should, we have the hope of God's grace (1 John 3:19–21). Through God's grace and by the Spirit, we are empowered to love others as Christ has loved us.

Through God's grace and by the Spirit, we are empowered to love others as Christ has loved us.

Questions

HOW DOES CHRIST'S LOVE FOR US IMPACT OUR LOVE FOR OTHERS?

WHAT DOES IT LOOK LIKE TO LOVE IN ACTION AND TRUTH?
HOW CAN YOU DO THIS PRACTICALLY IN YOUR LIFE?

HOW DOES KNOWING THAT GOD IS GREATER THAN OUR HEARTS
GIVE US ASSURANCE WHEN OUR HEARTS CONDEMN US?

WEEK 47 / DAY 4

1 John 4 *Practice this week's memory verse.*

LOVE IS THE DOMINATING THEME IN THE BOOK OF 1 JOHN, AND WE KNOW THIS TO BE TRUE AS JOHN BRINGS UP THIS THEME AGAIN IN 1 JOHN 4.

Lest these believers forget, love is at the heart of the gospel, and believers live out the gospel through their love for others. As they live out this love, they will be assured that they are genuine followers of Christ. Before speaking on the topic of love, John takes a moment to address incorrect theology. Those who departed from the truth do not believe that Jesus Christ came from God in the flesh. They do not affirm that Jesus was also God and the fulfillment of the promised Messiah.

Such beliefs do not align with the truth of the gospel. In order to die on the cross and forgive sin, Jesus had to be both fully man and fully God. True believers listen to and believe the truth of the gospel, but those who listen to and believe what the world says over the truth of the gospel do not know Jesus. Therefore, the believers John is writing to could have assurance that they belong to God because they confess the truth of who Jesus is.

In addition to confessing the truth of the gospel, believers also respond to the gospel through actions of love. John teaches us in verse 8 that God is love. God is the very definition of love, and therefore, we cannot truly love others if we do not know the God of love. As in the previous chapter, John provides an example of God's love. We have witnessed God's love in the way He sent His Son to us. Even though we were sinful and wayward, God loved us so much that He sent Jesus to die in our place and give us life.

Because God loved us in such a way, we are to love others. As believers, God's love for us should flow out of our lives. We are not to keep God's love to ourselves; we are to share His love through our words and actions. John writes in verse 12 that if we love others, we have assurance that we belong to God. Even on the day of judgment, we have no reason to fear because we have received God's love through Christ (1 John 4:17–18). Such truth gives us unshakeable confidence and peace.

God is the very definition of love.

Questions

WHAT KEEPS YOU FROM LOVING OTHERS? HOW CAN THE GOSPEL BREAK DOWN THESE BARRIERS SO THAT YOU CAN LOVE OTHERS?

HOW DOES JOHN GIVE ASSURANCE TO BELIEVERS IN 1 JOHN 4:13–16?

HOW DOES KNOWING THERE IS NO FEAR IN LOVE GIVE YOU CONFIDENCE?

WEEK 47 / DAY 5

1 John 5 *Practice this week's memory verse.*

JOHN HAS BEEN ENCOURAGING THIS GROUP OF BELIEVERS WITH THE TRUTH OF THE GOSPEL AND THE REALITIES OF GOD'S BLESSINGS THROUGH CHRIST.

As he finishes his letter, John leaves the church with some final words of comfort. If there are some who still doubt their salvation, these last words could provide the assurance they need to feel secure in their faith.

In verses 1–3, John presents two affirmations that may sound familiar to you. The first is that genuine believers are not only God's children but also show they are God's children through their love for others. The second is that genuine believers demonstrate their love for both God and others through their obedience to God's commands. Once again, John reveals how obedience and love are essential qualities of believers.

In verses 4–13, John provides hope for believers by teaching how believers in Christ are conquerors. The believers John is writing to are conquerors in that they have remained rooted in the truth. They could have followed the false teachers who left the church, but they essentially conquered these teachers by refusing to be swayed by them. Similarly, believers conquer the world by choosing to remain committed to Christ and the truth of the gospel. Unlike the false teachers, believers confess and affirm that Jesus is the Christ, who made salvation possible through His sacrifice. By His grace, God has caused followers of Christ to believe His testimony about who Jesus is and what He has done on the cross. This belief results in eternal life. However, those who reject God's testimony do not have this gift of eternal life.

John declares in verse 13 that his purpose in writing to these believers is that they have confidence that they have eternal life. As he ends his letter, John provides more truth to grant more assurance. John reminds believers that God hears and answers our prayers. He reiterates how believers do not continue in habitual sin, and he declares that believers are kept in God's hands and out of the grip of the enemy. Finally, he teaches that Jesus has granted belief in believers, enabling them to have a relationship with God. If we are in Christ, we are promised eternal life and security, strength to fight against sin, and an intimate relationship with our Father. May these truths comfort our hearts and ignite assurance in our faith.

Questions

HOW DOES KNOWING THAT GOD HEARS AND ANSWERS
YOUR PRAYERS ENCOURAGE YOU TO PRAY?

HOW HAS YOUR STUDY OF 1 JOHN ENCOURAGED
OR CHALLENGED YOU IN YOUR FAITH?

WEEK 47 / DAY 5

End-of-Week Reflection

Think back on all of the Scripture that you read and studied this week as you answer the questions below.

WHAT DID YOU OBSERVE ABOUT GOD AND HIS CHARACTER?

WHAT DID YOU LEARN ABOUT THE CONDITION OF MANKIND AND YOURSELF?

HOW DOES THIS WEEK'S SCRIPTURE POINT TO THE GOSPEL?

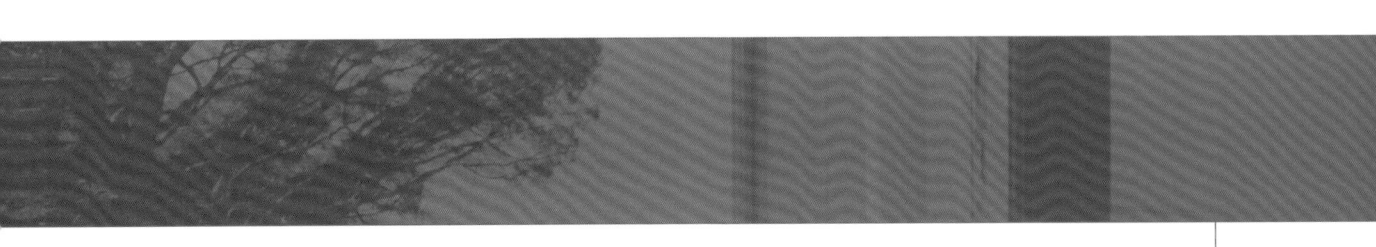

HOW DO THE TRUTHS YOU HAVE LEARNED THIS WEEK ABOUT GOD, MAN, AND THE GOSPEL GIVE YOU HOPE, PEACE, OR ENCOURAGEMENT?

HOW SHOULD YOU RESPOND TO WHAT YOU READ AND LEARNED THIS WEEK?
Write down one or two specific action steps you can take this week to apply what you learned. Then, write a prayer in response to your study of God's Word.

Week Forty-Seven Application

Before we begin a new week of study, take some time to apply and share the truths of Scripture you learned this week. Here are a few ideas of how you could do this:

- Schedule a meet-up with a friend to share what you are learning from God's Word.

- Use these prompts to journal or pray through what God is revealing to you through your study of His Word.

    — LORD, I FEEL...

    — LORD, YOU ARE...

    — LORD, FORGIVE ME FOR...

    — LORD, HELP ME WITH...

- Spend time worshiping God in a way that is meaningful to you, whether that is taking a walk in nature, painting, drawing, singing, etc.

- Paraphrase the Scripture you read this week.

_____
_____
_____
_____
_____
_____
_____
_____
_____
_____
_____
_____

- Use a study Bible or commentary to help you answer questions that came up as you read this week's Scripture.

- Take steps to fulfill the action steps you listed on Day 5.

- Use highlighters to mark the places you see the metanarrative of Scripture in one or more of the passages that you read this week. (See *The Metanarrative of Scripture* on page 14.)

Believers are to pursue and remain in the truth of God's Word amid false teaching.

THE BOOK OF
2 John

DATE WRITTEN

c. AD 85–95

AUTHOR

The Apostle John wrote this letter along with 1 and 3 John. He was a devoted disciple of Jesus who witnessed His death and resurrection. At the time he wrote this letter, John was an elder in the church, leading a community of house churches around the city of Ephesus.

AUDIENCE

This letter is written to "the elect lady and her children" (2 John 1). Most scholars believe this refers to a local church rather than a person. The cultural influences of Ephesus likely prompted John to encourage these believers in their faith and to exhort them in love, truth, and obedience to the Lord.

HISTORICAL CONTEXT

John wrote this letter during an intense period of persecution for the church. Many scholars believe John did not address anyone by name in the event the letter was intercepted by Roman officials. Despite the threat of persecution, John encourages these churches to stand firm in the gospel.

GENRE

Epistle

KEY WORDS

Love, Truth, Obedience

THEMES

1. Christians can walk in obedience as they love one another.

2. The Church should beware of deceivers who promote a false gospel.

KEY VERSE

This is love: that we walk according to his commands. This is the command as you have heard it from the beginning: that you walk in love.
—2 John 6

Week Forty-Eight Memory Verse

"I am the Alpha and the Omega," says the Lord God, "the one who is, who was, and who is to come, the Almighty."

REVELATION 1:8

WEEK 48 / DAY 1

2 John
Practice this week's memory verse.

RECEIVING INSTRUCTION AND ENCOURAGEMENT IS HELPFUL, BUT HAVING THAT INSTRUCTION AND ENCOURAGEMENT REITERATED ALLOWS THOSE TRUTHS TO DEEPEN IN OUR MINDS AND HEARTS.

The book of 2 John continues the same purpose as 1 John, rejecting false teaching while affirming what is true for followers of Christ. Some view 2 John as a "cover letter" of sorts that may have been read before 1 John was read. Whether or not this is the case, 2 John presses into the truth that believers are to pursue and remain in the truth of God's Word amid false teaching.

The author, the Apostle John, reminds the church he is writing to of the truth they know and believe—the truth of the gospel. It is in this truth that the believers need to remain. In fact, John writes in verse 4 how glad he is to hear how those in the church are walking in the truth. Doing so keeps the church from becoming swayed by false teachers. These false teachers do not confess that Jesus is the Christ, who came in the flesh, thus denying His sacrificial atonement on the cross. If Jesus did not take on flesh, then He could not have shed His blood for us on the cross. And if Jesus was not the Christ, He would not have conquered sin and death through His death and resurrection. Those who deny these essential truths deny the gospel and therefore are not true believers.

Believers, however, confess these truths and remain rooted in these truths. John warns believers in verse 9 not to go beyond the teaching of the gospel. This means that we are not to pursue teaching that denies or adds to the gospel. Instead, we are to remain in Christ's teaching by clinging to the truths of the gospel and rejecting anything that contradicts those truths. In verses 10–11, John writes not to welcome false teachers. This may seem surprising since Scripture calls us to be hospitable (1 Peter 4:9). However, we must understand the context of this admonition. Those who greeted and hosted people in the first century essentially blessed those they hosted and affirmed their support of them to the community. Therefore, hosting and greeting false teachers would imply support of their teaching. In fact, doing so would even be considered sharing in those teachers' evil works (2 John 11). While believers are to be kind to false teachers, they are to remain unsupportive of and uninvolved in their teaching.

John then ends his short letter by expressing his desire to come and visit these believers in person, face to face (2 John 12). Though this letter is short, it contains important reminders for both John's original audience and for us today. As we read these verses, may we take them to heart so that we, too, can be known as those who walk in the truth (2 John 4).

Questions

WHAT DOES JOHN SAY REMAINS WITH US IN VERSE 2?
HOW DOES THIS ENCOURAGE YOU?

ACCORDING TO VERSE 6, HOW IS LOVE DISPLAYED IN BELIEVERS?
WHAT DOES THIS PRACTICALLY LOOK LIKE?

HOW CAN YOU GUARD YOURSELF AGAINST FALSE TEACHING
AND REMAIN IN CHRIST'S TEACHING?

THE BOOK OF
3 John

DATE WRITTEN	c. AD 85–95
AUTHOR	The Apostle John wrote this letter in addition to 1 and 2 John. In it, he refers to himself as "the elder," specifying his position as an elder in the church. A fellow believer, Demetrius, likely brought the letter to Gaius.
AUDIENCE	Written to an individual named Gaius (3 John 1:1), John addressed the opposition Gaius faced from Diotrephes. Gauis was possibly a pastor of a local church under the authority of the Apostle John, and John wrote to provide counsel in this difficult situation.
HISTORICAL CONTEXT	This letter focuses on the relationship between two individuals, making it a very personal letter. However, the relational dynamics between Gaius and Diotrephes were common within the early church and even today. John's letter provides Christians with a greater understanding of how to live in accordance with God's Word through the Spirit.
GENRE	*Epistle*
KEY WORDS	*Truth, Testify, Good*
THEMES	1. Christians must remain steadfast in faith by following God's Word, even in the face of opposition. 2. Believers can serve God by supporting the work of ministry.
KEY VERSE	*Dear friend, do not imitate what is evil, but what is good. The one who does good is of God; the one who does evil has not seen God.* —3 John 11

WEEK 48 / DAY 2

3 John
Practice this week's memory verse.

TODAY, WE COME TO THE FINAL INSTALLMENT OF THE APOSTLE JOHN'S THREE LETTERS.

Along with the Gospel of John, these letters were likely written in Ephesus before John was imprisoned on the island of Patmos, where he would write the book of Revelation. In this third correspondence, John addresses his dear friend, Gaius, and the trouble he faced from a man named Diotrephes. Through this situation, John provides believers with a practical example of how to remain faithful despite hostility and opposition.

At first glance, 3 John might seem like an odd addition among all the theologically rich books of the New Testament. It is conversational in nature and addresses a specific person and their situation. But as we study, we quickly see how this letter builds on all John shared in 1 John and 2 John. If you remember, 1 John taught us to remain faithful, heed true doctrine, and live in obedience. The book of 2 John then built on these basics of our faith as John addressed how believers must walk in truth and love. Now, here in 3 John, like a pastor giving us a real-life example in a sermon, John uses Gaius's struggles to help us learn how to walk in truth.

The word "true" or "truth" is used seven times in this short book of 3 John (CSB). John commends Gaius for his testimony of walking in truth and "in a manner worthy of God" (3 John 6). Gaius practically did this through his support of missionaries who traveled from town to town, sharing the gospel. But he also faced prideful opposition and selfish ambition from Diotrephes. Diotrephes slandered Gaius and other believers and withheld support from missionaries. In 3 John 11, John tells Gaius not to imitate evil but to imitate good because "The one who does good is of God." In other words, Gaius must not give in to the same behaviors as Diotrephes but instead imitate the truth of the gospel.

And what is the truth? Jesus succinctly defines truth for us in John 17:17. In His prayer to the Father on our behalf, He says, "Sanctify them by the truth; your word is truth." When believers walk in the truth of Scripture, they walk in a manner worthy of God. No matter what opposition or suffering comes, we rest in the truth of God's Word, the truth of God's faithfulness, and the truth of His promises fulfilled in Christ.

Questions

READ THE VERSES BELOW. WHAT DO THEY TEACH BELIEVERS ABOUT TRUTH?

John 1:14

John 8:31–32

John 14:6

John 17:19

IN WHAT WAYS CAN YOU IMITATE GOOD INSTEAD
OF EVIL IN THE FACE OF SLANDER?

HOW DO 1, 2, AND 3 JOHN BUILD UPON EACH OTHER? HOW DO THESE LETTERS
ENCOURAGE YOU TO WALK "IN A MANNER WORTHY OF GOD" (3 JOHN 6)?

We contend for the faith as we await the joyful day we stand in the presence of our Savior.

THE BOOK OF
Jude

DATE WRITTEN	c. AD 60–80
AUTHOR	Jude, the author of this small epistle, was Jesus's half-brother and the brother of James. Jude was not a disciple of Jesus during His earthly ministry but later believed after Jesus's resurrection (John 7:5, Acts 1:14).
AUDIENCE	Jude's audience is debated. With the heavy use of Jewish references, many believe that Jude wrote to Jews who became believers, but some speculate that he wrote in order to inform Gentile believers about Jewish customs. Either way, this letter addressed those who are called by Christ (Jude 1). This letter is for all believers.
HISTORICAL CONTEXT	Possibly written to the church in Antioch, the believers there were infiltrated by false teachers. Jude wrote his letter to encourage believers to remain steadfast and vigilant in their faith, despite the false teachers' attempt to pervert the truth.
GENRE	*Epistle*
KEY WORDS	*Truth, Ungodliness, Obedience*
THEME	1. Christians must contend for the truth of the gospel of Jesus Christ with steadfast faith and perseverance. 2. Believers must guard against false teaching that promotes a message antithetical to the gospel.
KEY VERSE	*But you, dear friends, as you build yourselves up in your most holy faith, praying in the Holy Spirit, keep yourselves in the love of God, waiting expectantly for the mercy of our Lord Jesus Christ for eternal life.* —Jude 20–21

WEEK 48 / DAY 3

Jude
Practice this week's memory verse.

TODAY, WE COME TO JUDE, A SHORT LETTER WITH JUST TWENTY-FIVE VERSES.

In Jude's greeting, he states that he is a servant of Jesus and brother of James, who also penned a letter. Like James, Jude does not tell us he is Jesus's half-brother; we learn this elsewhere in Scripture, where he is called Judas—which is another name for Jude (Matthew 13:55, Mark 6:3). Though Jude and Jesus shared the same mother, Jude recognized he was a sinner saved by grace like everyone else. His posture toward Jesus is one of humility, not familial gain or fame. In his letter, Jude teaches fellow servants of Christ what it means to contend for, or defend, the faith among false teachers, as well as how to detect them.

Jude states in verse 3 that he is eager to write about the salvation he shares with fellow believers. But because ungodly, false teachers have infiltrated the church, Jude instead writes about how to recognize false teachers and the dangerous behaviors that accompany them. Jude's use of multiple Old Testament examples confirms that his original audience was familiar with the Scriptures. Each example in the following verses reminds believers that judgment awaits those false teachers who are marked by blatant sin and disobedience.

Jude begins by mentioning the rebellion after the Exodus, the fallen angels, and Sodom and Gomorrah. With these examples, he displays how we must be on guard against unbelief, pride, and perversion. In Jude 10, we read, "But these people blaspheme anything they do not understand." In other words, false teachers simply follow their desires like animals and ignore the truth of the gospel. Further, Jude mentions Cain, Balaam, and Korah. These men were each selfish, discontent, and rebellious. As if these traits were not enough, Jude shares specific illustrations concerning how false teachers hide in the sea like reefs that sink ships, operate as selfish shepherds, and act like waterless clouds, fruitless trees, and wandering stars. They grumble, they are arrogant, and they use people. They do not display the character of Christ.

These warnings from Jude are timeless truths believers must heed even today. Though the ungodly will be punished, they can still wreak havoc within our churches if we are not vigilant. We battle against these false teachers by building up our faith, praying in the Spirit, growing in our love of God, displaying mercy, and expectantly waiting for Christ's return. We contend for the faith as we await the joyful day we stand in the presence of our Savior.

Questions

THOUGH JUDE WAS A HALF-BROTHER OF JESUS, HE HUMBLY INTRODUCES HIMSELF, NOT BY HIS FAMILIAL CONNECTION BUT AS "A SERVANT OF JESUS CHRIST AND A BROTHER OF JAMES" (JUDE 1). *Why is his posture toward Jesus so important?*

WHAT DO FALSE TEACHERS LOOK LIKE IN OUR CHURCHES TODAY? HOW DOES JUDE'S LETTER HELP YOU IDENTIFY THEM?

HOW CAN YOU BE VIGILANT AGAINST FALSE TEACHERS WITHIN YOUR CHURCH AND AMONG FELLOW BELIEVERS? WHAT PRACTICAL STEPS CAN YOU TAKE IN EACH OF THE CATEGORIES BELOW?

Building up your faith:

Praying in the Spirit:

Growing in your love for God:

Displaying mercy:

Waiting expectantly for Christ:

> We serve the Alpha and Omega—the Creator of the universe, the One who is and was and is to come.

THE BOOK OF Revelation

DATE WRITTEN	c. AD 90–95
AUTHOR	John, the author of the Gospel of John and 1, 2, and 3 John wrote Revelation. John was exiled to the island of Patmos when he received the Revelation.
AUDIENCE	Revelation was written to seven churches in Asia Minor—Ephesus, Smyrna, Pergamum, Thyatira, Sardis, Philadelphia, and Laodicea. The churches in Asia Minor were threatened by persecution and false teaching. Revelation was written as a message of hope for these Christians, displaying the glory of Christ and His coming eternal victory. Revelation transcends time in its message of hope to believers.
HISTORICAL CONTEXT	At the time John received the Revelation, Jerusalem had been destroyed (c. AD 70), Christians faced intense persecution within the Roman empire, and believers longed for Christ's return. Exiled himself, John recorded the glorious victory of Jesus Christ, the destruction of all sin and evil, and the unimaginable beauty of the new heaven and new earth. Though times seemed dark then, as they do even today, hope reigns because Jesus sits on His throne awaiting the day He returns for His bride, the Church.
GENRE	*Epistle, Prophecy*
KEY WORDS	*Lamb, Heaven, Throne*
THEMES	1. One day, Christ will return to consummate His kingdom and all things will be made new. 2. Evil will not triumph forever.
KEY VERSE	*Then I saw a new heaven and a new earth; for the first heaven and the first earth had passed away, and the sea was no more. I also saw the holy city, the new Jerusalem, coming down out of heaven from God, prepared like a bride adorned for her husband.* —Revelation 21:1–2

WEEK 48 / DAY 4

Revelation 1 *Practice this week's memory verse.*

IF WE ARE HONEST WITH OURSELVES, IT IS LIKELY THAT WE HAVE NEGLECTED THE BOOK OF REVELATION FOR FEAR OF DIFFICULTY AND A LACK OF UNDERSTANDING.

However, this revelation from John is incredibly important, for it describes Jesus's final victory over Satan. When we feel as if evil is winning, when our circumstances seem hopeless, Revelation reminds us that God authors the end of our story, and the end of our story is good.

Most scholars agree that the Apostle John penned Revelation. John is the beloved disciple of Jesus and author of the fourth Gospel. He writes Revelation while stranded on the island of Patmos, likely where Rome exiled political prisoners. While on Patmos, John receives an incredible vision from Christ, detailing the last piece of God's redemption plan: ridding the world of sin. John pens Revelation not as an author but as a translator or a recorder. Jesus is the primary author of Revelation, and this book is His comfort to the seven churches in Asia Minor and to us.

In John's vision, he recognizes Jesus, but His appearance is not the same as when John first knew Him. Jesus unveils His true form as the glorious King of kings. His hair shines white as wool, symbolizing the fullness of wisdom. His eyes are like a blazing fire, seeing and knowing all. His feet are like bronze, unshakable and strong. Out of His mouth comes a double-edged sword, symbolizing the power of His Word (Revelation 1:12–16).

Throughout this chapter, you may notice that the word "seven" is repeated eleven times. Bible scholars call seven the number of perfection. It symbolizes divine origin and authority. Therefore, the repetition of the number seven communicates the credibility of John's message. In addition to communicating the divine origin and authority of his vision, John also reminds the churches in Asia Minor that Jesus is near. To understand this, let us look specifically at the golden lampstands. These lampstands represent the seven churches of Asia Minor to whom Jesus is speaking. Where is Jesus found in John's vision? He is standing in the midst of the lampstands, or standing in the midst of His churches (Revelation 1:13). At the time of John's letter, the Asian churches were riddled with persecution. John's message reminds them that Jesus is near.

Like the Asian churches, we too can take comfort in Revelation. We serve the Alpha and Omega—the Creator of the universe, the One who is and was and is to come. Jesus reigns. And His kingdom is coming. We need not fear the dark. Revelation reminds us that the light is coming.

Questions

WHAT IS YOUR EXPERIENCE WITH THE BOOK OF REVELATION? HAVE YOU READ IT BEFORE? WHY OR WHY NOT? *Take a moment to jot down questions you have so far, what you hope to learn, or what makes you nervous about diving into Revelation.*

READ REVELATION 1:12–13. JOHN CALLS JESUS "THE SON OF MAN." THIS WAS THE PRIMARY TERM THAT JESUS USED TO DESCRIBE HIMSELF. READ MATTHEW 9:6, MATTHEW 26:64, MARK 8:31, AND LUKE 18:31. *Why might Jesus use this term to describe Himself? (Hint: read Daniel 7:13–14 for help.) Why might John describe Jesus in this way?*

USING THE DIAGRAM BELOW, COMPARE AND CONTRAST JESUS'S PRESENTATION WHILE ON THE EARTH AND HOW HE REVEALS HIMSELF IN REVELATION. *How is He similar, and how is He different? For help, read Isaiah 53.*

WEEK 48 / DAY 5

Revelation 2 *Practice this week's memory verse.*

CAN YOU IMAGINE IF JESUS GAVE SPECIFIC INSTRUCTIONS TO YOUR LOCAL CHURCH? LIKELY, YOU AND YOUR FELLOW CHURCH MEMBERS WOULD BE QUICK TO TAKE ACTION.

In Revelation 2–3, Jesus, in the radiance of heaven, gives specific affirmations and condemnations to the seven churches of Asia Minor. These instructions serve as both comfort and warning for these churches and for modern churches as well. Jesus's words remind the churches that the day of the Lord is near, and Christians should be ready. In chapter 2, Jesus addresses the churches in Ephesus, Smyrna, Pergamum, and Thyatira.

First, Jesus addresses the church in Ephesus. Jesus sees this church's toil and endurance through persecution and false teaching. But in this endurance, their love for the gospel has dwindled, and with it, their love for one another has dwindled, too. Christ calls them to return to the passionate faith they once had.

Next, Jesus speaks to the church in Smyrna. Jesus does not rebuke this church but encourages them to persevere through current and future persecution. But though their trials will be fierce, the reward for their endurance is worth the fight—a crown of life and eternity spent with Jesus.

Jesus then addresses the church in Pergamum. Jesus affirms their steadfastness through persecution but condemns their inconsistent faith. At the time of John's letter, Pergamum was a hub for pagan religion and idol worship. Thus, Jesus says this region is "where Satan's throne is" and where Satan lives (Revelation 2:13–14). Some members of the Pergamum church were mixing the gospel with false teaching.

And finally, at the end of this chapter, Jesus speaks to the church in Thyatira. This church boasts opposite strengths of the church in Ephesus, for Jesus praises Thyatira's love for one another. However, He condemns members of the church who fell prey to the seduction of a local prophetess. Jesus calls her "Jezebel," referencing the wife of King Ahab, who led Israel from God and into idol worship (1 Kings 16:29–32). In the same way, the prophetess was leading Christians into sexual immorality and pagan praise.

Throughout Jesus's messages, He does not condemn a city without a call to repentance. These addresses to His churches are out of love and mercy, desiring for them the fullness of faith so that they may dwell with Him in glory. As believers in the modern church, we, too, should heed Jesus's warnings. Like the churches in Revelation, we are prone to wander, prone to mix our faith with the world's wisdom, and prone to worship false gods. Let us, too, be ready for Jesus's coming as a bride prepares for her groom.

Questions

IF YOU HAD TO DESCRIBE EACH OF THE CHURCHES IN TODAY'S READING IN ONE WORD, WHAT WORD WOULD YOU CHOOSE?

Ephesus	*Smyrna*	*Pergamum*	*Thyatira*

HOW DO JESUS'S ENCOURAGEMENTS AND WARNINGS TO THE CHURCHES COMMUNICATE HIS LOVE AND MERCY TOWARD HIS PEOPLE?

WEEK 48 / DAY 5

End-of-Week Reflection

Think back on all of the Scripture that you read and studied this week as you answer the questions below.

WHAT DID YOU OBSERVE ABOUT GOD AND HIS CHARACTER?

WHAT DID YOU LEARN ABOUT THE CONDITION OF MANKIND AND YOURSELF?

HOW DOES THIS WEEK'S SCRIPTURE POINT TO THE GOSPEL?

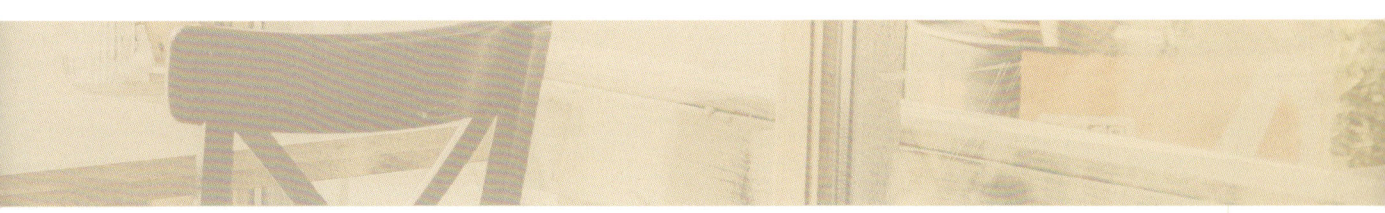

HOW DO THE TRUTHS YOU HAVE LEARNED THIS WEEK ABOUT GOD, MAN, AND THE GOSPEL GIVE YOU HOPE, PEACE, OR ENCOURAGEMENT?

HOW SHOULD YOU RESPOND TO WHAT YOU READ AND LEARNED THIS WEEK?
Write down one or two specific action steps you can take this week to apply what you learned. Then, write a prayer in response to your study of God's Word.

Week Forty-Eight Application

Before we begin a new week of study, take some time to apply and share the truths of Scripture you learned this week. Here are a few ideas of how you could do this:

- Schedule a meet-up with a friend to share what you are learning from God's Word.
- Use these prompts to journal or pray through what God is revealing to you through your study of His Word.

— LORD, I FEEL...

— LORD, YOU ARE...

— LORD, FORGIVE ME FOR...

— LORD, HELP ME WITH...

- Spend time worshiping God in a way that is meaningful to you, whether that is taking a walk in nature, painting, drawing, singing, etc.

- Paraphrase the Scripture you read this week.

_____
_____
_____
_____
_____
_____
_____
_____
_____
_____
_____
_____
_____
_____

- Use a study Bible or commentary to help you answer questions that came up as you read this week's Scripture.

- Take steps to fulfill the action steps you listed on Day 5.

- Use highlighters to mark the places you see the metanarrative of Scripture in one or more of the passages that you read this week. (See *The Metanarrative of Scripture* on page 14.)

Week Forty-Nine Memory Verse

I heard every creature in heaven, on earth, under the earth, on the sea, and everything in them say, Blessing and honor and glory and power be to the one seated on the throne, and to the Lamb, forever and ever!

REVELATION 5:13

WEEK 49 / DAY 1

Revelation 3 *Practice this week's memory verse.*

I KNOW YOUR WORKS. THIS STATEMENT UNITES THE THREE MESSAGES REMAINING IN JESUS'S ADDRESS TO THE CHURCHES IN ASIA MINOR (REVELATION 3:1, 8, 15).

"I know your works" is both an encouragement and a warning, for we know that Jesus knows all, sees all, and is never absent from our lives. However, because Jesus knows our deeds, He holds us accountable for every sin we commit. In Revelation 3, Jesus continues His encouragements and warnings to the churches in Sardis, Philadelphia, and Laodicea.

Addressing the church in Sardis, Jesus beckons them to wake up from their spiritual slumber and be alert. He alludes to their history here, for the city had been captured twice by enemy forces. Jesus compares Sardis to a watchman who has fallen asleep on his post. But this church is not without hope, for Jesus sees a faithful few in Sardis who can facilitate repentance and revival in the city.

Jesus then speaks to the church in Philadelphia. He commends their faithful endurance, despite facing obstacles of false teaching and persecution. Jesus does not give this church a rebuke but instead an invitation into His kingdom or "the new Jerusalem" (Revelation 3:12). For them, there is "an open door" (Revelation 3:8), for they have not wavered in their affections. Jesus encourages this church to press on despite difficulties and keep their eyes fixed on the reward awaiting them in heaven.

And finally, for the church in Laodicea, Jesus reserves the harshest criticism. He does not have any praise for this church. The city of Laodicea was known for its economic success and wealth, and this prosperity diminished the church's desire for Christ. Jesus describes their apathy as lukewarm water, serving no purpose for practical use. Ironically, in Laodicea's pride, they are more in need than ever. Jesus calls them "wretched, pitiful, poor, blind and naked" (Revelation 3:17). But even so, Jesus extends grace to this wayward church. Jesus disciplines, not as a critical overlord but as a loving father, desiring the best for His children. Jesus calls them to return to His love, for He is waiting for them to simply open the door, invite Him in, and rekindle their relationship.

Though Christ's messages to His churches vary in intensity, one thing remains constant—Jesus desires His churches to draw near to Him. Jesus's words to the seven churches look a lot like God's pursuit of Israel, a consistent call to forgetful people to remember their Redeemer. This is grace. Though Christ's Church wavers in faithfulness, His own love never wavers. Christ's love is sure.

Questions

LOOK AT THE OPENING SENTENCE OF EACH OF THE MESSAGES TO CHRIST'S CHURCHES IN REVELATION 2–3. HOW DOES JESUS DESCRIBE HIMSELF IN EACH ONE? *What do these descriptions teach you about Jesus's reign in heaven and over creation?*

IF YOU HAD TO DESCRIBE THE CHURCHES IN TODAY'S READING IN ONE WORD, WHAT WORD WOULD YOU CHOOSE?

Sardis	*Philadelphia*	*Laodicea*

REREAD JESUS'S MESSAGES TO THE SEVEN CHURCHES. IF YOU HAD TO PICK A MESSAGE THAT MOST APPLIES TO YOU, WHICH ONE WOULD YOU PICK? WHY? WHAT IS JESUS'S APPLICATION FOR YOU?

WEEK 49 / DAY 2

Revelation 4 *Practice this week's memory verse.*

AFTER JESUS GIVES JOHN THE MESSAGES TO THE CHURCHES OF ASIA, HE BECKONS HIM AGAIN WITH ANOTHER VISION.

This time, Jesus invites John into the heavenly throne room of God. Before we dive into what John sees, let us look at Revelation 4 in the context of the entirety of John's vision. Chapters 4 and 5 showcase God and the Lamb (Jesus) in majestic glory, worthy of praise and honor. The splendor of God's throne room, the perfection of His judgment, and the obedience of the Lamb (Revelation 5) prepare our hearts to read the coming judgment of evil and the restoration of the world throughout the remainder of Revelation.

In heaven, John sees God upon His throne in full radiance and grandeur. He is so magnificent that John can only describe Him in terms of the most precious and valuable gemstones of the day—jasper and carnelian. Twenty-four elders encircle God's throne (Revelation 4:4). Some scholars believe the elders encircling God's throne are people, while others believe they are angels. If people, scholars suggest that these twenty-four elders represent the twelve tribes of Israel and the twelve disciples of Jesus. And finally, around God's throne are four winged creatures. Scholars differ on what these creatures may symbolize, but most agree that these creatures represent some form of God's created order: perhaps wild beasts (the lion), domesticated animals (the ox), humans (the man), and creatures of the air (the eagle). The description of these creatures is similar to those described around God's throne in Isaiah 6, Ezekiel 1, and Daniel 7. No matter what these creatures represent, their most important feature is their unending worship of God.

John's vision is not only filled with sights of wonder but the sounds of heaven as well. The creatures and the elders utter continuous praise before God. Their praise reminds us of the entire point of Revelation and of our lives as Christians—to magnify God as the one true God and Christ as King. Revelation 4 calls our hearts to share in the same worship as the creatures and the elders around God's throne, for we do not have to wait for eternity to sing "Holy, holy, holy." As we continue in Revelation, we are to hold tight to the majesty of chapter 4, for the song that surrounds the throne of God is the song that the earth was always meant to sing. It is the song of the coming glory that will fill the air when Christ's kingdom meets earth in His return.

Questions

ON A SCRAP SHEET OF PAPER, TAKE A MOMENT TO TRY AND ILLUSTRATE JOHN'S DESCRIPTION OF HEAVEN. THIS DOES NOT HAVE TO BE A MUSEUM-WORTHY PIECE OF ARTWORK, BUT INSTEAD, THIS EXERCISE IS MEANT TO HELP YOU BETTER UNDERSTAND THE MAJESTY OF HEAVEN AND OF GOD.
If you are uncomfortable drawing, instead list out the descriptions of God and His throne room.

WHAT DOES THE SPLENDOR OF GOD'S THRONE ROOM COMMUNICATE TO YOU ABOUT GOD? HOW DOES THIS LEAD YOU TO WORSHIP?
For more descriptions of God's throne room, refer to Isaiah 6:1–4 and Ezekiel 1:22–28.

DO YOU REGULARLY SIT IN AWE OF GOD, HIS CHARACTER, AND HIS MAJESTY? HOW MIGHT YOU MAKE THIS A MORE REGULAR PART OF YOUR FAITH?

WEEK 49 / DAY 3

Revelation 5 *Practice this week's memory verse.*

JESUS IS THE ONE WHO ACCOMPLISHED GOD'S WILL AND, THEREFORE, DESERVES THE UTMOST HEAVENLY HONOR.

Revelation 5 presents a visual of Jesus's accomplishment and His resulting glory. Seeing a vision of heaven's throne room, the disciple John witnesses a scroll in the hand of the Lord God Almighty. Words fill the front and back of the scroll, and seven seals hide its contents. According to a biblical scholar, the scroll is a symbol of God's divine will (Sproul, 2311). It may generally refer to God's covenant, Law, plans for His people, or purposes for the world.

This symbol alludes to Daniel 12:4, when an angel relayed to the prophet Daniel the events surrounding Christ's second coming. The angel informed Daniel that these events would be concealed in a book until the end of the age.

Now, in a vision that represents the end of the age, it is time to open the book, or scroll, in Revelation. Opening the scroll symbolizes both revealing and realizing the words written. But John acknowledges that there is no one to do so. In other words, John knows that no human is righteous enough to enter God's sacred presence. No human is pure enough to come before God's power and holiness and take the scroll from His hand. Such a person would have to be equal to God in His divine authority and have the supernatural ability to accomplish God's will.

Then, one of the elders, or members of the heavenly council, assures John that there is Someone who can break the seals. He says, "Do not weep. Look, the Lion from the tribe of Judah, the Root of David, has conquered so that he is able to open the scroll and its seven seals" (Revelation 5:5). Suddenly, a Lamb approaches God's throne. The Lamb seems dead but is alive; this image describes Jesus, who died for our sins yet rose from the grave, defeating the kingdom of evil. The Lamb has seven horns and seven eyes, which represent the fullness of power and holiness upon Jesus through God's Spirit.

Because Jesus accomplished redemption for God's people, He is worthy to take the scroll. As God in the flesh, Jesus was the only human able to fulfill the plan of salvation and, therefore, He is the only One able to fulfill the events for the end of the age. With God's divine will in Christ's hands, the elders, creatures, and angelic hosts of heaven erupt in praise.

Questions

HOW DOES THIS VISUAL LEAD YOU TO MARVEL AT CHRIST?

IN WHAT WAYS DO YOU SEE THE LORD'S FAITHFULNESS REFLECTED IN THIS PASSAGE?

IF WE BELIEVE THAT CHRIST IS THIS PROMISED SAVIOR, WE CAN LOOK FORWARD TO THE DAY WHEN WE WILL JOIN THE ANGELIC HOSTS AND PROCLAIM THAT ONLY HE IS WORTHY. *How does this truth impact your daily living?*

WEEK 49 / DAY 4

Revelation 6 *Practice this week's memory verse.*

TROUBLES OCCUR IN THE TIME LEADING UP TO CHRIST'S RETURN, BUT JESUS IS STILL IN CONTROL.

Revelation 6 conveys various visions of catastrophes that indicate the end of the age, which is the indefinite period between Christ's ascension to heaven and His second coming. In the Lord's sovereignty, catastrophes are instruments for God's good purposes.

It is important to note that God is not the author of evil. Evil in the world is the product of man's rebellion against the Lord, which began in the garden (Genesis 3). Nevertheless, evil is not greater than God's power. Because He controls all things, God does not allow evil to operate outside of His will. He seizes the wicked schemes of human and spiritual beings and directs them toward goodness in the end. We see this truth in the four horsemen of Revelation 6.

As the Lamb opens the first four seals on the scroll, four horsemen ride across the scene. The first horseman, with his bow and crown, represents nations who seek to conquer other nations. The second horseman, on a red horse and carrying a sword, represents war, violence, and bloodshed. The third horseman, riding a black horse and possessing a pair of scales in his hand, represents famine and inflation as a result of food shortages. Finally, the fourth horseman, riding a pale green horse, represents death.

The picture of the Lamb opening the seals, along with the appearance of each horseman, indicates Jesus's authority over destructive powers. Jesus removes His restraining hand and unleashes the horsemen, allowing them to wreak havoc. But He does so according to His just character. As He gives the world over to destruction, Jesus is also enacting His righteous judgment on wickedness.

Though His judgment rains on the wicked, God shelters the faithful from the storm. We recognize this truth when Jesus unlocks the fifth seal. Once this seal is open, John sees the souls of the persecuted under an altar. The souls cry out to God and ask Him to punish their oppressors. Then, the souls are clothed in white robes, mirroring the righteousness of their Savior. They are given rest in God's presence, for they know God will make all things right in His time.

The martyred followers of Christ find eternal refuge under the protection of the Holy One, while the opening of the sixth seal brings destruction to the natural world. The whole earth is shaken, causing all people to shudder before the just God. But those who place their faith in Jesus can have unfaltering hope.

Questions

HOW DO THE IMAGES IN REVELATION 6 IMPACT
YOUR VIEW OF TROUBLES IN THIS LIFE?

WHAT DID YOU LEARN ABOUT GOD'S CHARACTER
FROM TODAY'S PASSAGE?

HOW DOES THIS PASSAGE PROVIDE COMFORT IN CATASTROPHE?

WEEK 49 / DAY 5

Revelation 7 *Practice this week's memory verse.*

GOD SHIELDS HIS SERVANTS FROM JUDGMENT AND SECURES THEM IN HIS PRESENCE.

In Revelation 6, we discussed how the end of the age involves catastrophes and calamities. Now, in Revelation 7, we learn how God preserves His people through these difficult times so that they can worship Him forever.

After the Lamb opens six seals on the scroll, there is a pause. The focus shifts from the seventh and final seal to the people of God who have endured natural disasters and the four horsemen's chaos. A sense of reprieve follows ruin. John sees four angels who hold back the winds as if they are preventing further disturbance on the earth. They follow the instruction of another angel who says, "Don't harm the earth or the sea or the trees until we seal the servants of our God on their foreheads" (Revelation 7:3). Full destruction does not consume the world's wickedness until every faithful follower of God bears His seal.

To understand the implications of this seal, it helps to first understand the significance of a seal in the ancient world. Often, a seal was used to display ownership and authority. Some commentators have noted how slave owners would mark their slaves or servants with a seal on their foreheads to show to whom these servants belonged. Other commentators have compared the seal in this chapter to a royal signet ring, which was used to authenticate official letters from a person of authority or to show their ownership of a particular item. With this historical context, we can understand the seal of God as a symbol of God's protection and possession of His people. And we can ultimately understand this event in chapter 7 as an answer to the question asked at the end of chapter 6. Amid the chaos and calamity of the first six seals being removed, the people of the earth asked "And who is able to stand?" in Revelation 6:17. The answer comes in this chapter: the servants of God—those marked by the seal—are able to stand and endure to the end. This seal carries with it a promise of God's protection, which we will see more fully expressed in Revelation 9:4.

Revelation 7 totals the number of these servants of God to 144,000. Some scholars believe that the figure 144,000 is symbolic of wholeness and completion, while others believe it literally refers to 144,000 Jewish Christians. Either way, the number captures the fact that God will preserve all of His people in faith; no one will be forgotten or left behind. Furthermore, He will seal His servants from all nations. God will protect all of us in Christ from present calamities, claim us as His own, and lead us to worship before His throne.

Questions

READ MATTHEW 28:19–20. HOW IS THIS VERSE
RELATED TO REVELATION 7:9–10?

BASED ON REVELATION 7:16–17,
HOW WILL GOD SATISFY US IN HIS PRESENCE?

WEEK 49 / DAY 5

End-of-Week Reflection

Think back on all of the Scripture that you read and studied this week as you answer the questions below.

WHAT DID YOU OBSERVE ABOUT GOD AND HIS CHARACTER?

WHAT DID YOU LEARN ABOUT THE CONDITION OF MANKIND AND YOURSELF?

HOW DOES THIS WEEK'S SCRIPTURE POINT TO THE GOSPEL?

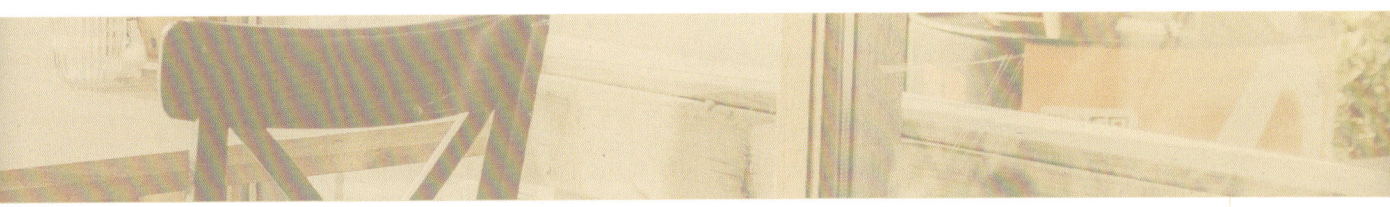

HOW DO THE TRUTHS YOU HAVE LEARNED THIS WEEK ABOUT GOD, MAN, AND THE GOSPEL GIVE YOU HOPE, PEACE, OR ENCOURAGEMENT?

HOW SHOULD YOU RESPOND TO WHAT YOU READ AND LEARNED THIS WEEK?
Write down one or two specific action steps you can take this week to apply what you learned. Then, write a prayer in response to your study of God's Word.

Week Forty-Nine Application

Before we begin a new week of study, take some time to apply and share the truths of Scripture you learned this week. Here are a few ideas of how you could do this:

- Schedule a meet-up with a friend to share what you are learning from God's Word.
- Use these prompts to journal or pray through what God is revealing to you through your study of His Word.

— LORD, I FEEL...

— LORD, YOU ARE...

— LORD, FORGIVE ME FOR...

— LORD, HELP ME WITH...

- Spend time worshiping God in a way that is meaningful to you, whether that is taking a walk in nature, painting, drawing, singing, etc.

- Paraphrase the Scripture you read this week.

_____
_____
_____
_____
_____
_____
_____
_____
_____
_____
_____
_____
_____

- Use a study Bible or commentary to help you answer questions that came up as you read this week's Scripture.

- Take steps to fulfill the action steps you listed on Day 5.

- Use highlighters to mark the places you see the metanarrative of Scripture in one or more of the passages that you read this week. (See *The Metanarrative of Scripture* on page 14.)

Week Fifty Memory Verse

*The kingdom of the world has become
the kingdom of our Lord and of his Christ,
and he will reign forever and ever.*

REVELATION 11:15B

WEEK 50 / DAY 1

Revelation 8 *Practice this week's memory verse.*

SIN CORRUPTS THE NATURAL WORLD; THEREFORE, THE EARTH, WITH ALL OF HUMANITY, WILL EXPERIENCE THE CALAMITIES THAT LEAD UP TO CHRIST'S SECOND COMING.

When the first man and woman fell in Genesis 3, their rebellion created a cosmic shift in the universe. Brokenness impacted not only the heart of mankind but also the sky, land, and sea. As a result, all of creation has suffered, evidenced by earthquakes, storms, and floods. In Revelation 8, these natural disasters are signs of the end of the age.

Revelation 8 begins with the Lamb opening the seventh seal, which initiates the most intense round of calamities. Silence follows this opening, as if to highlight that the day of the Lord has come (Zephaniah 1:7) (Sproul, 2315). Then, seven angels with seven trumpets stand before God. Trumpets signify the Lord's victory. For instance, in the battle of Jericho, Israel's army marched around the city seven times and blew trumpets, and God brought down Jericho's wall so that the Israelites could settle in the Promised Land (Joshua 6). This event foreshadowed the victory the Lord had over evil through Jesus Christ. With His life, death, and resurrection, Jesus defeated sin and the grave; His defeat sounded like the blast of the loudest trumpet.

John then sees an eighth angel who fills an incense burner with fire and throws the flames on the earth. The fire causes thunder, rumblings, lightning, and an earthquake. But before he throws this fire to the earth, this angel offers incense to represent the prayers of the saints. This offering conveys that, in the midst of catastrophe, God hears and remembers His people.

The angels with trumpets prepare to blow their instruments. With the sound of the first trumpet, hail and fire burn a third of the earth and trees. This disaster singes all green grass. The second angel blows his trumpet, and a mountain, burning with fire, is tossed into the sea, destroying a third of the sea creatures and ships. At the third trumpet, a blazing star falls into a third of the rivers and springs, making the water toxic. The fourth angel ushers in calamity for the sun: a third of the light emanating from the sun, moon, and stars darkens.

These images of natural destruction may also be symbols of the destruction of the wicked. It is likely that these pictures serve as representations of the world's fallenness that will be purified through Christ's judgment and renewed through His mercy. And all those in Christ are recipients of this mercy. Though the events of Revelation can be difficult to read, believers can ultimately rest in the mercy of Christ, knowing that "the sufferings of this present time are not worth comparing with the glory that is going to be revealed to us" (Romans 8:18).

Questions

READ ROMANS 8:18–25. HOW DO THESE VERSES INFORM YOUR UNDERSTANDING OF REVELATION 8?

HOW DOES GOD SHOW MERCY IN REVELATION 8:6–12?

WRITE A PRAYER TO GOD THAT YOU CAN RECALL WHILE NAVIGATING THE STORMS OF LIFE.

WEEK 50 / DAY 2

Revelation 9
Practice this week's memory verse.

IN TODAY'S READING, WE CONTINUE TO WITNESS GOD'S JUDGMENT UNFOLD UPON AN UNREPENTANT WORLD.

Yesterday, we learned that the seventh seal brought forth seven trumpets, which would release the worst calamities unveiled thus far in increasing intensity. In today's chapters, the fifth and sixth trumpets are blown, also known as the first and second woes.

An angel blows the fifth trumpet, and a star falls from heaven to earth (Revelation 9:1). Most scholars identify this star with a personality of some kind, either a man or an angel. Some even identify the star as Satan. God gives him the key to the abyss (Revelation 9:1–2). Scholars believe this abyss, or bottomless pit, is the holding location for demonic forces and perhaps the "beast" mentioned later in Revelation. Out of the abyss rises smoke and an army of terrifying, human-like locusts. God permits these locusts to torment unrepentant humans with painful stings. Depending on the interpretation of Revelation, some scholars believe these will be legitimate locusts, some believe they represent historical military forces, and yet some others view these locusts as symbols of other threats—likely modern warfare or demonic forces.

After the sixth trumpet is blown, God allows the release of four fallen angels who were bound in punishment in the Euphrates River. These angels call forth a demonic army of two hundred million who kill a third of the human race with the fire, smoke, and sulfur from their mouths. Some scholars believe that these demons carry out mass casualties by deceiving human armies into violent war with one another. No matter their methods of destruction, the fifth and sixth trumpets remind us that even Satan and demonic activity are under the sovereign authority of God, for no evil force can operate without God's foreknowledge.

The chapter closes with sobering words. The remainder of mankind, the two-thirds who survive the locusts and the demonic attacks, do not repent and return to the Lord, even after witnessing such pervasive destruction (Revelation 9:20–21).

These trumpets may have triggered your memory, as they sound eerily similar to the plagues God poured out on the Egyptians as a result of their hardened hearts (Exodus 7–11). From the Old Testament to the New Testament, God has not changed. His wrath burns against those who refuse Him, but His love is steadfast for those who call Him their Father. As He redeemed the Israelites from Egypt and brought them to the Promised Land, He will soon bring His children to the ultimate Promised Land (Revelation 22).

Questions

REREAD REVELATION 9:1–2 AND JOB 1:6–12. GOD GIVES THE "FALLEN STAR" THE KEYS TO THE ABYSS, AND GOD ALLOWS SATAN TO STRIKE JOB — BUT ONLY WITHIN HIS LIMITS. *What does this tell you about God's control over evil in the world? How does this encourage you?*

IN REVELATION, GOD IS BOTH MERCIFUL AND WRATHFUL AGAINST SIN. HOW CAN GOD BE BOTH MERCIFUL AND WRATHFUL AT ONCE? HOW DOES GOD DISPLAY HIS MERCY TOWARD THOSE WHO TRUST IN HIS SON FOR SALVATION?

THE END OF REVELATION 9 TELLS US THAT THE EVIL IN THE WORLD DID NOT REPENT AND TURN FROM THEIR WAYS. WHAT DOES THIS TEACH YOU ABOUT MANKIND? WHAT SIN CAN YOU CONFESS TO GOD TODAY SO THAT YOU CAN AVOID THIS MISTAKE? *Write a prayer of repentance to God.*

WEEK 50 / DAY 3

Revelation 10 *Practice this week's memory verse.*

BETWEEN THE SIXTH AND THE SEVENTH TRUMPETS, JOHN SEES A MIGHTY ANGEL DESCEND FROM HEAVEN.

The appearance of this angel symbolizes God's faithfulness to His people and His authority over creation. Above his head is a rainbow, God's symbol of mercy (Genesis 9:12–17). His legs are pillars of fire, the element God used to guide His people throughout their Exodus from Egypt (Exodus 13:21–22). His voice is like that of a roaring lion. And when he speaks, John hears the sound of "the seven thunders" (Revelation 10:4), signaling a coming storm, the seventh and most violent trumpet. This angel did not come in destruction but in divine mercy. The angel comes to commission John to bring Jesus's message to many peoples, nations, languages, and kings (Revelation 10:11).

The angel announces that there will "no longer be a delay" in God's coming judgment (Revelation 10:6), and soon, Christ's kingdom will finally be established on earth. But in the meantime, God instructs John to take a scroll from the angel's hand and eat it. This instruction is similar to the instruction given to Ezekiel in Ezekiel 3, for he, too, was commissioned to bring a message of warning and repentance to the hard-hearted Israelites. The eating of the scroll symbolizes a deeper level of digesting God's words. Like Ezekiel, John physically experiences the bitterness of God's wrath and tastes the sweetness of His mercy for those grafted into His family (Revelation 10:9–10). And we know both men were obedient to deliver their messages, for we have the testimony of their faithfulness in our hands as we read the Bible today. Through John's obedience, God shares His plan of redemption with generations to come.

Right between the blasts of the two most intense expressions of God's wrath (the sixth and seventh trumpets), we find a commission for John to warn and encourage mankind with his vision. God's desire to share details of the coming judgment is hope for those in Christ and grace to unbelievers. His warning sparks a natural fear that should fill the Christian's heart with the necessary urgency to see friends, families, and neighbors come to saving faith. We should not delay. The time to believe is now, for there is great hope for us amidst these terrifying judgments. Those in Christ will be ushered into His kingdom, where hope is fulfilled, peace is plentiful, and joy is abundant.

Questions

WHAT DEFINING CHARACTERISTICS OF GOD ARE SYMBOLIZED BY THE ANGEL'S APPEARANCE IN REVELATION 10:1–5? (HINT: READ GENESIS 1, GENESIS 9:13–16, EXODUS 13:21–22, EXODUS 34:29, AND JOB 37:4.)

WHY MIGHT THE SCROLL INGESTED BY JOHN BE SWEET IN HIS MOUTH BUT BITTER IN HIS STOMACH (REVELATION 10:9–11)?

WHAT IS THE SIGNIFICANCE OF THE ANGEL DELIVERING A MESSAGE OF WARNING AND ENCOURAGEMENT BETWEEN THE SIXTH AND SEVENTH TRUMPETS? WHAT DOES THIS COMMUNICATE ABOUT GOD'S LOVE FOR US?

WEEK 50 / DAY 4

Revelation 11 *Practice this week's memory verse.*

THE INTERPRETATION OF REVELATION CAN BE A POINT OF DISSENSION AMONG SOME BELIEVERS.

But no matter how you approach this challenging book, one truth remains consistent: the kingdom of the world becomes the kingdom of our Lord and of His Christ (Revelation 11:15). Like chapter 10, chapter 11 is an interlude that takes place between the sixth and seventh trumpets. And by the end of this chapter, the fateful seventh trumpet will blow, ushering in the final display of God's wrath.

Before the final trumpet blares, two actions take place. First, God instructs John to take measurements of His temple. Some scholars believe that John measures a future, physical reconstruction of the temple in Israel, while others believe that the temple is a symbol for believers in Christ's Church. Either way, John does not only measure the dimensions of the building, as is customary in his time, but he also numbers the people as well. God is keeping a count of His people, showcasing His safekeeping and ownership of His royal priesthood (1 Peter 2:9).

Second, God commissions two martyrs to prophesy the coming destruction and call the world to repentance. They wear sackcloths (a physical sign of repentance) and receive the ability to perform signs and miracles from God, similar to the plagues that Moses brought upon Egypt (Exodus 7–11). Unfortunately, when the martyrs finish their ministry, they will be captured and murdered by "the beast." Scholars believe this beast refers to the antichrist, whom we will learn more about when we study Revelation 13. Though the martyrs die and suffer public humiliation, God raises them to glory three and a half days later.

Who are these martyrs? Views differ among scholars. Some commentators believe that these are two human beings that God will commission, while some believe them to be true Christians during the time of papal power, or the time leading up to the Reformation. Others believe that these two martyrs represent the Church, while still others believe them to be either Moses and Elijah or Enoch and Elijah, standing boldly before enemies on behalf of God. No matter who these martyrs are, they remind us of God's patience and grace to provide a call of repentance in the final days.

And finally, the seventh trumpet blasts. Before we see the final trumpet's effects on earth in the coming chapters, we read about the effects of the seventh trumpet in heaven. Upon its sound, heaven erupts in worship. Christ's kingdom is finally coming to earth. The elders and angels in heaven anticipate the coming victory. By the end of Revelation 11, God's wrath is coming to completion, and Jesus's kingdom is closer than ever.

Questions

READ MATTHEW 18:20 AND MARK 6:7. WHY DID JESUS SEND OUT HIS DISCIPLES IN GROUPS OF TWO? BASED ON WHAT YOU HAVE LEARNED, WHY DOES GOD SEND THE MARTYRS IN GROUPS OF TWO? *What does this teach you about the importance of Christian community?*

WHAT IS THE ARK OF THE COVENANT MENTIONED IN REVELATION 11:19? TO FIND OUT, READ EXODUS 25:10–22. *Why do you think that John saw the ark of the covenant exposed in heaven before the seventh trumpet's calamity begins?*

READ REVELATION 11:15. NOW READ REVELATION 21:1–4 AND REVELATION 21:22–27. HOW DOES THE KINGDOM OF THE WORLD DIFFER FROM THE KINGDOM OF GOD AND OF CHRIST? *Why should this spark joy in the hearts of believers?*

WEEK 50 / DAY 5

Revelation 12 *Practice this week's memory verse.*

UPON A FIRST READ, REVELATION 12 CAN SEEM LIKE A MYSTICAL FAIRYTALE, COMPLETE WITH ANGELS BATTLING A DRAGON AND EVEN A MYSTERIOUS CLIFFHANGER.

But if we dig a little deeper, we uncover beautiful imagery simultaneously telling the story of Israel and of Christ's Church—a wayward, persecuted people redeemed by Christ. At the end of chapter 11, an angel blew the seventh trumpet, ushering forth the last and most severe display of God's wrath, called the seven bowls (Revelation 15). However, before the bowls of judgment are poured, Revelation depicts ongoing spiritual warfare. In fact, throughout the blowing of the trumpets, spiritual warfare on earth gradually increases. But now the warfare has come to a head.

In this chapter, we observe three main characters: a dragon, a woman, and a child. The dragon symbolizes Satan (Revelation 12:9). Commentators differ on the identity of the woman; some believe she represents national Israel, and others believe she represents the true Church. And the child, born of the woman and the enemy of the ancient serpent, is Jesus.

With these characters in mind, we can begin to see the story of Israel and the story of Christ's redemption woven throughout the chapter. For example, Israel (the woman) is pregnant with hope, the hope of a coming Savior. But Satan cannot devour this Messiah. Instead, the Messiah ascends to reign at the right hand of God. This is the gospel, the good news that our Savior triumphs over the dragon. Secondly, this woman is driven into the wilderness, where God tenderly cares for her.

In this chapter, we see Satan defeated twice—once when he is unable to devour the Son and another time when he is thrown from heaven to earth. Satan's defeat is not just a future promise; it has already begun. It started when Jesus rose from the grave, and it will end when Satan is finally thrown into the lake of fire (Revelation 20:10). Until then, the dragon carries out his frustration among God's people on earth, "prowling around like a roaring lion, looking for anyone he can devour" (1 Peter 5:8). Though there is more destruction to come, as God's angels proclaim, the devil "knows his time is short" (Revelation 12:12). Soon, God will dwell with His people for all eternity (Revelation 21).

Questions

TAKE A MOMENT TO REREAD REVELATION 12:4–5, DEPICTING THE SON OF THE WOMAN ESCAPING THE JAWS OF THE DRAGON. HOW DOES THIS COMMUNICATE THE STORY OF THE GOSPEL? HOW DOES THIS GIVE YOU HOPE?

HOW DOES THE WOMAN'S STORY IN THIS CHAPTER MIRROR THE STORY OF GOD'S CHOSEN PEOPLE ISRAEL? *In the middle of describing God's wrath, why might Jesus remind His people of God's faithful provision?*

WEEK 50 / DAY 5

End-of-Week Reflection

Think back on all of the Scripture that you read and studied this week as you answer the questions below.

WHAT DID YOU OBSERVE ABOUT GOD AND HIS CHARACTER?

WHAT DID YOU LEARN ABOUT THE CONDITION OF MANKIND AND YOURSELF?

HOW DOES THIS WEEK'S SCRIPTURE POINT TO THE GOSPEL?

HOW DO THE TRUTHS YOU HAVE LEARNED THIS WEEK ABOUT GOD, MAN, AND THE GOSPEL GIVE YOU HOPE, PEACE, OR ENCOURAGEMENT?

HOW SHOULD YOU RESPOND TO WHAT YOU READ AND LEARNED THIS WEEK?
Write down one or two specific action steps you can take this week to apply what you learned. Then, write a prayer in response to your study of God's Word.

Week Fifty Application

Before we begin a new week of study, take some time to apply and share the truths of Scripture you learned this week. Here are a few ideas of how you could do this:

- Schedule a meet-up with a friend to share what you are learning from God's Word.
- Use these prompts to journal or pray through what God is revealing to you through your study of His Word.

— LORD, I FEEL...

— LORD, YOU ARE...

— LORD, FORGIVE ME FOR...

— LORD, HELP ME WITH...

- Spend time worshiping God in a way that is meaningful to you, whether that is taking a walk in nature, painting, drawing, singing, etc.

- Paraphrase the Scripture you read this week.

_____
_____
_____
_____
_____
_____
_____
_____
_____
_____
_____
_____
_____

- Use a study Bible or commentary to help you answer questions that came up as you read this week's Scripture.

- Take steps to fulfill the action steps you listed on Day 5.

- Use highlighters to mark the places you see the metanarrative of Scripture in one or more of the passages that you read this week. (See *The Metanarrative of Scripture* on page 14.)

Week Fifty-One Memory Verse

Lord, who will not fear and glorify your name? For you alone are holy. All the nations will come and worship before you because your righteous acts have been revealed.

REVELATION 15:4

WEEK 51 / DAY 1

Revelation 13 *Practice this week's memory verse.*

WHO IS LIKE THE LORD? THIS QUESTION IS REPEATED OVER AND OVER THROUGHOUT SCRIPTURE (EXODUS 15:11, PSALM 89:8, PSALM 113:5).

There is only one true God who created the heavens and the earth. He is holy, powerful, righteous, and our only Savior. But in Revelation 13, Satan deceives the people of the planet with counterfeits to salvation and demands that all the earth worship the beasts.

The chapter begins with a beast rising from the sea. There is some debate about who this beast represents. Some have interpreted the beast as the antichrist (1 John 2:22) or the man of lawlessness (2 Thessalonians 2:3–12). Others have interpreted the beast as political leaders or world powers that are against the Lord and His church (Daniel 7). Still others say that the first beast represents the Roman Empire, and the second beast represents Nero, whose name adds up to 666 in Hebrew characters. Whoever the first beast is, he is given power for a time, and the earth worships him, saying, "Who is like the beast? Who is able to wage war against it?" (Revelation 13:4). He blasphemes yet is worshiped by the world, while Christians are persecuted and face martyrdom (Revelation 13:7–10). Yet God does not abandon His people, and the faithfulness of Christians will be part of the eventual defeat of the dragon (Revelation 12:11, 15:2).

In verse 11, another beast rises from the earth. This beast performs signs and wonders, deceiving the world and making the earth worship the first beast. The people who follow him are given a seal, whether physical or spiritual in nature, and no one can buy or sell without the marking of the beast. Anyone who refuses to worship the image of the beast is to be killed.

The beasts of Revelation 13 may seem powerful, but they use counterfeit signs that imitate the one true God. For example, the first beast has overcome a mortal wound, similar to Jesus, who overcame the grave. The second beast seals the people with a number, like God, who seals His children with the Holy Spirit (Revelation 7:1–4). The beasts have power, a throne, and authority, like God, but they are no match for God. Our God is incomparably stronger, and one day, He will have the final victory over Satan, defeating sin and death and destroying the evil beasts forever.

Questions

IN LIGHT OF REVELATION 13:10, READ 2 CORINTHIANS 4:16–18. WHAT WOULD IT LOOK LIKE FOR YOU TO FAITHFULLY ENDURE THE TRIALS OF YOUR LIFE? BE SPECIFIC.

FOR US AS CHRISTIANS, THERE WILL BE SUFFERING AND PERSECUTION IF WE FOLLOW JESUS. THE ENEMIES OF GOD WILL SEEK TO SILENCE AND HURT US. *Yet Christ has overcome the world (John 16:33), and He will have victory over every enemy. Does this truth scare you or encourage you? Why?*

DO YOU KNOW GOD WELL ENOUGH TO RECOGNIZE COUNTERFEITS OF HIM? HOW CAN YOU KNOW GOD AND HIS CHARACTER BETTER?

WEEK 51 / DAY 2

Revelation 14 *Practice this week's memory verse.*

IN HIS SECOND COMING, JESUS WILL DEDICATE BELIEVERS TO WORSHIP, BUT HE WILL DEDICATE THOSE WHO REFUSE HIS SALVATION TO WRATH.

In Revelation 7, we read about the 144,000—which some scholars consider a symbolic number for all of God's servants who have faith in Christ and bear His Spirit, while others believe it to be literally 144,000 Jewish Christians. In chapter 7, the Lord gathered His servants from every nation and clothed them in white. Their white robes represented spiritual cleansing: Jesus's blood shed on the cross paid for their sins and washed away corruption. As a result, the servants became priests. They entered God's presence, served at His throne, and worshiped His name.

Revelation 14 returns to the 144,000. The 144,000 stand with the Lamb on Mount Zion, the hill in Jerusalem, which serves as a holy resting place for God's people. Each person has the name of the Lamb and the Father written on his or her forehead (Revelation 14:1). This mark signifies that they belong to the Lord. In the heavenly council, the servants do not fear judgment or punishment. Rather, they respond to their salvation with joy and praise. Together, they sing a song to their God. Revelation 14:3 says that only the 144,000 can learn this song; it is a personal melody for those whom God has redeemed and risen from the grave. Through their faith in the Lamb's sacrifice, the servants bear the Son's righteousness.

This picture of worship among the 144,000 in Revelation 14 conveys the destiny of all believers. Bearing the image of Jesus the High Priest, we will reflect His purity and blamelessness. We will rest on His mountain, serve in God's presence, and sing a song that only the redeemed hearts know.

While believers are set apart for life with the Lamb, the wicked are set apart for destruction with the beast. After his vision of the 144,000, John sees three angels flying and proclaiming announcements. The third angel says that if anyone worships the beast and bears its mark on his or her forehead, then he or she will face God's wrath. God's wrath describes His just anger toward evil. Those who idolize the beast join in its evil ways. They reject God's forgiveness and cleansing through the Lamb. Therefore, in His holy anger, Jesus, the One seated on the cloud in Revelation 14:14, will gather these participants of the kingdom of darkness and give them over to perish in sin.

Questions

TODAY WE LEARNED ABOUT A SONG THAT ONLY THE 144,000 COULD LEARN. WHILE WE DO NOT YET KNOW THIS SONG, WE CAN STILL WORSHIP GOD. *What song can you sing to the Lord today? Spend some time reflecting on its lyrics.*

IN WHAT WAYS DOES THIS PASSAGE MOTIVATE YOU TO SHARE THE GOSPEL WITH UNBELIEVERS?

WHERE DO YOU SEE GOD'S JUSTICE IN THIS PASSAGE?

WEEK 51 / DAY 3

Revelation 15 *Practice this week's memory verse.*

THE CATASTROPHES AT THE END OF THE AGE ARE TEMPORARY, AND GOD'S PEOPLE ARE SURE TO COME THROUGH THEM VICTORIOUSLY.

Though the present time is like walking barefoot on rocky terrain, we can be confident that God will give our feet rest. Since we are His, God will preserve our faith in Christ so that we can overcome this world's troubles and enter His eternal presence.

As we have learned so far, God orchestrates cycles of judgments on the wicked, which we see through the seven seals, the seven trumpets, and now through the seven bowl judgments to be executed in the following chapter. These judgments will fall upon the immoral, rebellious, and irreverent people and institutions who seek to advance the kingdom of darkness. These cycles put pressure on evildoers to turn from their sin and cling to God for salvation, while also pointing to the Lord's holy wrath. John sees a sign that these judgments will come to an end. For example, he sees seven angels with seven plagues. This vision signifies the final cycle of judgment and will conclude the period of time when God expresses His wrath through catastrophes on earth (Revelation 15:1).

Furthermore, John sees a vision that God will deliver His people from the calamities of this age. Those who conquer the beast stand on a sea of glass. They have harps in their hands and sing the songs of Moses and of the Lamb.

This picture alludes to Exodus 15. God had just led the Israelites out of Egyptian slavery, and the people sang about their victory. Leading up to their miraculous escape from Egypt, God sent a cycle of plagues to Egypt so that Pharaoh would release the Israelites. These plagues also served as judgment for Egypt's idolatry and injustice. Under the pressure of the final plague, Pharaoh let the slaves go, but later, he decided to pursue the Israelites to the Red Sea. God rose the waves of the Red Sea, allowing the Israelites to escape on dry ground. But He brought the water down on Pharaoh's army, and the oppressors of God's people drowned in God's wrath.

Like the Israelites in Exodus, we, too, will be delivered from the ungodly kingdoms of this world. The Lord will preserve us in faith. And, through our faith in Christ, we will conquer sin and evil. By the Holy Spirit, we will continue to hope in eternity, even when catastrophes surround us, knowing that any present trouble will not last and is ultimately bringing us closer to the King. Darkness may pursue us, but in Jesus, God will give us safe passage to escape and will lead us to rest in His presence.

Questions

WHAT ATTRIBUTES OF GOD DO YOU NOTICE
IN THE SONG IN REVELATION 15:3–4?

READ EXODUS 15:1–18. HOW DOES THIS SONG POINT TO THE GOSPEL?

HOW DOES REVELATION 15 ENCOURAGE YOU?

WEEK 51 / DAY 4

Revelation 16 *Practice this week's memory verse.*

LIKE AN EARTHQUAKE FIRST TREMORS BEFORE CRACKING OPEN THE GROUND, THE SEALS AND THE TRUMPETS IN PREVIOUS CHAPTERS WERE THE WARNING TREMORS OF A COMING EARTHQUAKE: THE FULL FORCE OF GOD'S WRATH.

In chapter 16, the final judgment is poured out on our unrepentant world. These judgments are delivered in the form of plagues, much like the plagues that struck the unrepentant Egyptians in Exodus 7–11. However, the plagues in Exodus temporarily destroyed Egypt, while the plagues of the seven bowls destroy the world as we know it. But God does not pour out wrath flippantly or spontaneously. The seven bowls are poured out so that God can usher in Christ's kingdom—one that is permanent and perfect.

The seven plagues in this chapter signify total destruction. Throughout the first five bowls, God's wrath is displayed against mankind and the throne of the beast. Then, the sixth and seventh bowls are poured out. But to understand the significance of these final two bowls, we must first understand the significance of the Euphrates River and "Babylon the Great." In the book of Revelation, Babylon is a symbol of evil and the enemies of God. In Old Testament times, Babylon was indeed an evil empire that oppressed God's people, and its geography can help us understand the significance of the river mentioned in this chapter. As the historic Babylonian Empire rose to power, it depended upon the protection provided by the Euphrates River, which served as a natural barrier between Babylon and its opposing nations. However, when the sixth bowl dries up the Euphrates, Babylon no longer has its shield. With this natural barrier gone, the earth prepares for Armageddon—Satan's final battle against God—for the end of evil is coming soon.

Finally, upon the seventh bowl, heaven declares, "It is done!" (Revelation 16:17). The tremors give way to a mighty earthquake and storm, God's final act of wrath upon Babylon. Even into their destruction, those who are unrepentant curse God. Their refusal to repent shows the total depravity of the humans remaining on earth. But even assembled against God, Babylon is no match for the Lord of lords. Upon this mighty quake, the kingdoms of the world are destroyed and prepared for the coming of a new kingdom.

These demonstrations of God's wrath upon the world can be difficult to read. But we must remember that God's wrath does not negate His goodness. Instead, God's wrath against evil proves His goodness. God was faithful to provide a sacrifice for our sins through His Son, Jesus, and He will be faithful to deliver His people into the ultimate Promised Land—eternity in peace with our beloved Savior, Jesus.

Questions

TAKE A MOMENT TO READ 2 CHRONICLES 36:15–20. WHAT CRIMES DID BABYLON COMMIT AGAINST GOD'S PEOPLE? HOW DOES THIS HELP YOU UNDERSTAND THE SYMBOLISM OF BABYLON IN REVELATION?

WHY MUST THIS SIN-STAINED EARTH BE DESTROYED IN ORDER TO USHER IN CHRIST'S PERFECT KINGDOM? WHAT DOES THIS TEACH YOU ABOUT GOD AND HIS TOLERANCE FOR SIN?

READING ABOUT THE WRATH OF GOD ON AN UNREPENTANT WORLD REMINDS US THAT THE END IS GRIM FOR THOSE WHO REFUSE GOD. HOW DOES READING ABOUT GOD'S WRATH MOTIVATE YOU TO SHARE THE HOPE OF JESUS?
Who in your life are you praying for to accept Christ? Take a moment to pray for them.

WEEK 51 / DAY 5

Revelation 17 *Practice this week's memory verse.*

IN GENESIS 11:1–9, SCRIPTURE DETAILS AN ACCOUNT THAT IS COMMONLY REFERRED TO AS "THE TOWER OF BABEL" OR "THE TOWER OF BABYLON."

In this account, humans attempt to build a tower that reaches the heavens so that they might make a name for themselves and usurp God's authority. The quest for power becomes their idol. Because of their evil hearts, God scatters them and jumbles their languages. And from this story, the empire of Babylon finds its origin. Even in some of the earliest days of mankind's history, Babylon represented idolatry. And in Revelation 17, Babylon is personified as a prostitute who seduces her prey with false promises of affluence and pleasure. The prostitute has one central goal: to allure kingdoms away from God and into the hold of Satan.

As we have previously discussed, Babylon was an evil empire written about in the Old Testament, and the book of Revelation uses Babylon as a symbol of those who are enemies of God. At this point, it is helpful to note that interpreters differ when it comes to the specifics of what Babylon represents in the book of Revelation. Some believe that Babylon is identified with Rome or Jerusalem, while some believe it is representative of the Catholic Church. Others believe it represents a future religious and commercial entity, while still others believe Babylon symbolizes past, present, and future kingdoms that live in sin and persecute God's people. Regardless of how one may understand the meaning of Babylon in Revelation, we can all agree that Babylon represents evil in opposition to God and His kingdom.

In Revelation 17, an angel elaborates on the fall of Babylon announced by the seventh bowl in yesterday's chapter (Revelation 16:18–19). The angel tells John how and why the prostitute allures her victims. The prostitute's outer appearance is beautiful and affluent; she is dressed in "purple and scarlet, adorned with gold, jewels, and pearls" (Revelation 17:4). Though she may seem attractive, we see her sitting on the scarlet beast, which signifies her partnership with evil.

In John's vision, the angel informs him of the schemes of the prostitute and of the beast. The prostitute is described as seated among many waters, which describes the peoples, multitudes, nations, and languages that will fall prey to her seduction (Revelation 17:15). With her victims, she forms an army of powerful kingdoms and rulers who will join Satan in the final battle against God, called Armageddon (Revelation 16:16, 17:14). But ultimately, Satan's army is no match for Jesus, who claims full and final victory.

The prostitute promised pleasure, and she delivered pain. She offered riches and delivered ruin. Revelation 17 begs us, as followers of Christ, to ask ourselves, "What are we allured by?" Wealth, influence, sex, and power are common idols in our culture. But we know they are merely empty promises of Babylon and can never truly satisfy. We know what is true: Christ will conquer, and because He conquers, so do we. By His strength, given to us through His Holy Spirit, we have the power to turn our eyes away from Babylon—the evil and emptiness of this world—and toward Christ's kingdom of true beauty, unfading riches, and unfailing promise.

Questions

WHAT IS THE END RESULT OF THOSE CAPTIVATED BY THE PROSTITUTE? HOW MIGHT THIS CHAPTER BE A WARNING FOR GOD'S PEOPLE TO AVOID IDOLIZING THE PLEASURES OF THE WORLD?

TAKE A MOMENT TO CONSIDER HOW YOU ARE BEING ALLURED BY THE PLEASURES OF THE WORLD IN YOUR CURRENT SEASON. WRITE A PRAYER, ASKING THE HOLY SPIRIT FOR STRENGTH TO FLEE FROM THESE TEMPTATIONS.

WEEK 51 / DAY 5

End-of-Week Reflection

Think back on all of the Scripture that you read and studied this week as you answer the questions below.

WHAT DID YOU OBSERVE ABOUT GOD AND HIS CHARACTER?

WHAT DID YOU LEARN ABOUT THE CONDITION OF MANKIND AND YOURSELF?

HOW DOES THIS WEEK'S SCRIPTURE POINT TO THE GOSPEL?

HOW DO THE TRUTHS YOU HAVE LEARNED THIS WEEK ABOUT GOD, MAN, AND THE GOSPEL GIVE YOU HOPE, PEACE, OR ENCOURAGEMENT?

HOW SHOULD YOU RESPOND TO WHAT YOU READ AND LEARNED THIS WEEK?
Write down one or two specific action steps you can take this week to apply what you learned. Then, write a prayer in response to your study of God's Word.

Week Fifty-One Application

Before we begin a new week of study, take some time to apply and share the truths of Scripture you learned this week. Here are a few ideas of how you could do this:

- Schedule a meet-up with a friend to share what you are learning from God's Word.
- Use these prompts to journal or pray through what God is revealing to you through your study of His Word.

— LORD, I FEEL...

_____
_____
_____

— LORD, YOU ARE...

_____
_____
_____
_____

— LORD, FORGIVE ME FOR...

_____
_____
_____
_____

— LORD, HELP ME WITH...

_____
_____
_____
_____

- Spend time worshiping God in a way that is meaningful to you, whether that is taking a walk in nature, painting, drawing, singing, etc.

- Paraphrase the Scripture you read this week.

_____
_____
_____
_____
_____
_____
_____
_____
_____
_____
_____
_____
_____

- Use a study Bible or commentary to help you answer questions that came up as you read this week's Scripture.

- Take steps to fulfill the action steps you listed on Day 5.

- Use highlighters to mark the places you see the metanarrative of Scripture in one or more of the passages that you read this week. (See *The Metanarrative of Scripture* on page 14.)

Week Fifty-Two Memory Verse

Then the one seated on the throne said, "Look, I am making everything new." He also said, "Write, because these words are faithful and true."

REVELATION 21:5

WEEK 52 / DAY 1

Revelation 18 *Practice this week's memory verse.*

IN THE PREVIOUS CHAPTER, BABYLON WAS PERSONIFIED AS A PROSTITUTE; NOW, IN THIS CHAPTER, BABYLON IS PICTURED AS A GREAT CITY THAT HAS FALLEN.

As we learned yesterday, interpreters have many different approaches to understanding the significance of Babylon in Revelation, but we can all agree that Babylon represents evil. And in today's reading, we learn how this great city of Babylon will fall, revealing how the kingdoms of this earth will crumble, but God's kingdom remains.

The first voice that speaks to John in Revelation 18 is an angel who describes Babylon's evil. The city of Babylon is completely corrupt. It is described as a home for demonism, revealing how all that is evil taints this kingdom. The nations around this kingdom have been swayed by Babylon's evil. They have been captivated by Babylon's ways, participating in her sinful behavior and taking from her what benefits them.

A second voice speaks for the remainder of Revelation 18, this time explaining the judgment that Babylon will experience. But first, the voice calls for God's people to come out of Babylon (Revelation 18:4). This verse teaches how believers are to be set apart from the evil of this world. As God's people, we are to reject sin instead of sharing in the sins of others. Though we are to remove ourselves from sin in the present, we look forward to the day when God will bring us out of sin forever.

The judgment that Babylon will face is harsh, but this judgment speaks to the seriousness of sin. God does not ignore sin or allow sin to continue. God knows and sees the sins of Babylon, and He will punish Babylon for its sins. As the mighty judge, God will enact justice upon Babylon for its sins and the suffering it has caused for His people. Babylon may think herself a queen, but because of God's judgment, she will lose her status of glory. Her gain will be traded for loss and her nobility for humility.

The sinful people of this world will mourn the ruin of Babylon, but God's people will rejoice (Revelation 18:19–20). However, the people's mourning should challenge us to keep pursuing God's kingdom. Unlike these people, we should be careful as believers not to cling to the temporary kingdoms of this world and what they offer. Instead, let us pursue what is eternal and view God's kingdom as greater than any kingdom of this earth.

Questions

HOW IS THE JUDGMENT OF BABYLON FAIR?

HOW IS GOD'S JUSTICE EVIDENT IN REVELATION 18? HOW DOES GOD'S JUSTICE GIVE YOU HOPE FOR THE INJUSTICE THAT OCCURS TODAY?

REVELATION 18:10, 17, AND 19 DESCRIBE BABYLON BEING DESTROYED IN A SINGLE HOUR. HOW DO THESE VERSES REVEAL THE MOMENTARY NATURE OF THE KINGDOMS OF THIS WORLD? *How does this challenge you to not cling to what is temporary?*

WEEK 52 / DAY 2

Revelation 19 *Practice this week's memory verse.*

REVELATION 18 REVEALED THE TRAGEDY OF SINFUL BABYLON, BUT REVELATION 19 REVEALS THE TRIUMPH OF GOD'S PEOPLE.

As believers today, we rejoice when justice is executed and sin is conquered. The joy we have in the present over Christ's past conquering of sin and Christ's current victory over sin anticipates our joy to come. When the sinful kingdoms of this earth are permanently washed away, all of heaven will rejoice.

In verses 1–4, we receive details about this celebration. A voice shouts with joy, praising God for who He is. The voice declares God's salvation, glory, and power, and it rejoices over how God brought about just judgment upon the sinful world. These words of praise and celebration are followed by the twenty-four elders and the four living creatures falling down and worshiping the Lord. In verses 6–8, a voice continues to praise the Lord, this time over the marriage of the Lamb. This marriage involves God's Church (the bride) uniting with Christ (the bridegroom). Verse 9 refers to this occurrence as "the marriage feast of the Lamb." The celebration of this blessed union is greater than any wedding we could imagine. One day, God's people will be dressed in white, symbolizing their purity from sin, and they will be united with Jesus to be with Him forever.

Our Savior is our bridegroom, but He is also our mighty warrior. Verses 11–21 recount Christ's defeat over sin and evil. Once Jesus rode a donkey (Matthew 21:1–11, Mark 11:1–11, Luke 19:28–40, John 12:12–19), but now He rides a white horse. His majesty is declared not only by this majestic horse but by Him having a name that "no one knows except himself" (Revelation 19:12). Though His robes are dipped in blood, it is not the blood of His enemies but His own that He poured out on the cross. This is our conquering Savior, who is our "KING OF KINGS and LORD OF LORDS" (Revelation 19:16). He is the Word of God, and by the word of His mouth, He will bring about judgment upon the wicked.

Our conquering Christ will defeat all of those against Him. While this judgment is full of loss, it is gain for God's people. God promises to remove sin and restore our world back to a place of peace and righteousness, and this judgment is part of His plan of restoration. So, let us praise our Savior for what He will do one day, celebrating now as we anticipate the celebration to come.

Questions

WHAT ARE THE REASONS FOR GIVING GOD PRAISE IN TODAY'S PASSAGE? CONSIDER THE WORD "BECAUSE" IN THE CHAPTER.

WHY SHOULD WE GIVE GOD PRAISE FOR HIS JUDGMENT UPON EVIL?

REREAD VERSES 11–16. HOW IS CHRIST'S MAJESTY DISPLAYED IN THESE VERSES? HOW IS HIS POWER DISPLAYED?

WEEK 52 / DAY 3

Revelation 20 *Practice this week's memory verse.*

GOD HAS PLANS TO SET THIS BROKEN WORLD RIGHT, AND IN REVELATION 20, WE CONTINUE TO SEE GOD'S JUDGMENT UNFOLD UPON ALL THAT IS WICKED AND SINFUL.

In the previous chapter, the beast and its armies were defeated. Now, the ultimate beast is defeated—Satan. But before Satan is officially vanquished, he is bound for a thousand years and thrown into an abyss to be kept from deceiving the nations. While believers differ in their views on how and when this binding takes place (see the extra on page 220 for more about this), we can take comfort that God has complete control over Satan. Satan is not powerful enough to escape the hand of God. Like a roaring lion caught in a trap, Satan will be bound.

In verses 7–10, we see the final fate of Satan. After God's allotted time, Satan will be thrown into the lake of fire, as will all those who follow Satan's evil ways. This imagery of fire represents absolute peril and destruction. Satan will be no more. Knowing that this is Satan's fate comforts us as believers in the present. The evil that occurs in this world is disheartening, and our battle against Satan and his agents of darkness is fierce. But one day, our enemy will be officially defeated, and we will never again experience his wicked ways.

Satan's fate is one of destruction, but the fate of others will be different. In verses 4–5, John sees people sitting upon thrones. Among the people on the thrones are those who have been martyred for their faith. They once died for the sake of Christ, but now they have been resurrected and given a position of glory alongside Christ. Verse 6 boasts of God's salvation. These believers are rescued from the second death. They may have physically died, but they will never experience spiritual death because of their salvation in Christ. This is our hope as believers. Whether in life or in death, we belong to the Lord, and death has no power over us.

Sadly, there are people who will experience this second death. Verses 11–15 reveal the final judgment that will take place. Those whose names are in the book of life, believers in Christ, will be brought into glory. But those who reject Christ and the gospel will be cast away and eternally punished. This reality is sobering, but its truth leaves us with a choice—will we choose eternal life in Christ or death?

Questions

HOW DOES KNOWING SATAN'S FATE GIVE YOU
HOPE IN LIGHT OF SIN AND WICKEDNESS?

HOW IS GOD'S PROTECTION OF HIS PEOPLE EVIDENT IN THIS CHAPTER?

WHAT HOPE DO BELIEVERS HAVE IN LIGHT OF JUDGMENT DAY?
CONSIDER 1 JOHN 4:16–18 AS YOU ANSWER THIS QUESTION.

WEEK 52 / DAY 4

Revelation 21 *Practice this week's memory verse.*

WITH ALL SIN, DARKNESS, AND WICKEDNESS JUDGED AND REMOVED, GOD'S PLANS TO MAKE ALL THINGS NEW ARE FINALIZED.

As believers, we all long for the day when we will live in a world transformed, a world that is finally at perfect peace. Revelation 21 gives us a glimpse of what this world will be like. Revelation 21 is the culmination of all that we have hoped for as believers—it is the culmination of God's promises fulfilled.

In verses 1–8, we learn of two essential qualities of the new heaven and the new earth: peace and presence. Verse 1 tells us how the first heaven and earth have passed away, and verse 4 tells us how death, grief, crying, and pain are no more. God's promises to make all things new are now realized. Nothing taints or threatens to taint God's perfect creation. All is set right. All is made new. All is as it should be. The peace that the world once possessed before the Fall is restored, and God's people live in perfect rest.

This peace and rest are also connected with God's presence. Verses 3, 4, and 7 reveal the relationship God and His people have in eternity. As the new Jerusalem comes to meet earth, heaven and earth continue to collide as God comes to permanently dwell with His people. While there is a degree of separation between God and His people in the present, this separation will be removed in eternity. All those in Christ will dwell in the full presence of God and live with Him in His perfect creation forever.

Verses 9–27 also give us insight into what the new Jerusalem will look like. For the people of Israel, Jerusalem was a place of significance. It was a city of glory, especially because it was where the temple was and, therefore, where God's presence dwelled. However, the new Jerusalem will be unlike anything we could imagine. It will be a place of supreme glory and security, and its size will be astonishing. But perhaps what most significantly sets the new Jerusalem apart is that there is no temple because God and Christ fully dwell within it. Though the city is shaped like the Holy of Holies—the innermost part of the temple, where the Spirit of God dwelled—there is no separation between God and people in this place. As we learned in our study of Hebrews, only the high priest was able to enter the Holy of Holies, and he could only do so once a year. But God's presence will forever be with His people in the new Jerusalem. God's full glory will illuminate the whole city, and God's people will forever walk in this light.

Questions

WHAT DO GOD'S ACTIONS OF MAKING ALL THINGS NEW REVEAL ABOUT HIS CHARACTER?

HOW DOES VERSE 4 GIVE YOU HOPE IN TIMES OF SUFFERING?

READ ISAIAH 65:17–25. HOW DO YOU SEE THESE PROMISES FULFILLED IN REVELATION 21?

WEEK 52 / DAY 5

Revelation 22 *Practice this week's memory verse.*

IN REVELATION 21, WE RECEIVED A GLIMPSE OF WHAT THE NEW HEAVEN AND EARTH WILL LOOK LIKE, AND REVELATION 22 CONTINUES THIS REVELATION.

Verses 1–5 connect the images of peace and presence that the previous chapter contained. We see a flowing river coming from God's throne and running through the middle of the city. The tree of life is on each side of the river, bearing fruit and leaves that provide continual abundance and spiritual nourishment. These specific images point back to the garden of Eden, but they also fulfill prophecies such as Zechariah 14:8 and Ezekiel 47. Such prophecies fulfilled yet again reveal how God's promises have been fully realized.

In verses 3–5, we continue to see what life will look like for God's people. With God's presence fully dwelling on earth, God's people will see Him face to face. This is extremely significant as no human has been able to see God's face. But this will be the blessing for every follower of Christ. God's name will also be on our foreheads, signifying the intimate relationship we have with Him. As God's people, we will receive the special privilege of reigning with God, although it is God who ultimately reigns. Together, we will live happily in God's light and worship Him joyfully for eternity.

All of these blessings revealed in Revelation 21 and 22 seem too good to be true, but they are real indeed. The angel in verse 6 confirms how these words and revelations are faithful and true; therefore, they are worthy of being trusted. But lest we doubt, the voice of Jesus affirms these blessings and promises. In verses 7–20, Jesus proclaims how He is truly coming soon. He affirms how those who have been purified through His blood will inherit these blessings. But those who reject Christ and His gospel will be kept from experiencing and inheriting such gifts.

Yet Jesus offers an invitation right here and now for anyone who does not know Him to trust and believe in Him. Throughout this chapter, Jesus beckons us to come to Him, and He comforts all those who believe in Him with the truth that He is indeed coming soon. Just as Christ invites us to come to Him, so do we look forward to the day when He will return. Though the present is full of hardships, Jesus is coming soon. Therefore, let our hope and joy rise up as we look forward to the day when we will behold our Savior and forever dwell with Him.

Questions

HOW DOES VERSE 3 FULFILL GOD'S PROMISES?

HOW DOES KNOWING THAT JESUS IS COMING SOON COMFORT YOU?

WEEK 52 / DAY 5

End-of-Week Reflection

Think back on all of the Scripture that you read and studied this week as you answer the questions below.

WHAT DID YOU OBSERVE ABOUT GOD AND HIS CHARACTER?

WHAT DID YOU LEARN ABOUT THE CONDITION OF MANKIND AND YOURSELF?

HOW DOES THIS WEEK'S SCRIPTURE POINT TO THE GOSPEL?

HOW DO THE TRUTHS YOU HAVE LEARNED THIS WEEK ABOUT GOD, MAN, AND THE GOSPEL GIVE YOU HOPE, PEACE, OR ENCOURAGEMENT?

HOW SHOULD YOU RESPOND TO WHAT YOU READ AND LEARNED THIS WEEK?
Write down one or two specific action steps you can take this week to apply what you learned. Then, write a prayer in response to your study of God's Word.

Week Fifty-Two Application

As this study comes to a close, take some time to apply and share the truths of Scripture you learned this week and throughout the entire study. Here are a few ideas of how you could do this:

- Schedule a meet-up with a friend to share what you are learning from God's Word.
- Use these prompts to journal or pray through what God is revealing to you through your study of His Word.

  — LORD, I FEEL...

  _____
  _____
  _____

  — LORD, YOU ARE...

  _____
  _____
  _____

  — LORD, FORGIVE ME FOR...

  _____
  _____
  _____

  — LORD, HELP ME WITH...

  _____
  _____
  _____

- Spend time worshiping God in a way that is meaningful to you, whether that is taking a walk in nature, painting, drawing, singing, etc.

- Paraphrase the Scripture you read this week.

_____
_____
_____
_____
_____
_____
_____
_____
_____
_____
_____
_____
_____

- Use a study Bible or commentary to help you answer questions that came up as you read this week's Scripture.

- Take steps to fulfill the action steps you listed on Day 5.

- Use highlighters to mark the places you see the metanarrative of Scripture in one or more of the passages that you read this week. (See *The Metanarrative of Scripture* on page 14.)

Four Millennial Views

Many questions likely arise when considering details regarding the end of the world. While we cannot be entirely sure of all that will take place, this God-given curiosity drives us to the Creator of time—the One who has much to say about the end times in His Word.

The Lord has graciously revealed to us what is coming at the end of His redemptive story in Scripture. While there are many unknown details, we can be sure that God is victorious, and His people from all generations will be reunited with Him.

The most important event that will take place at the end of the world is the return of Christ. In Revelation 20, the Apostle John describes one-thousand years during which Jesus will reign over the earth. Many Christians refer to this time as "the millennium" or "the millennial kingdom." While the ultimate purpose of this passage in Revelation is to point us to the hope and security we have in Christ, there are many different beliefs regarding when and how this millennium will occur in relation to Jesus's second coming. Four major views held within the Church include amillennialism, postmillennialism, classical premillennialism, and dispensational premillennialism.

AMILLENNIALISM

Amillennialists believe that the millennium referenced in Revelation 21 is a figurative period of time—not a literal thousand-year kingdom. Amillennialists believe that this thousand-year period refers to the present age and that we currently live in the millennium. Christ is King, and He is reigning, but He is reigning from heaven. This period was inaugurated from heaven at His ascension, and it will be consummated at His second coming. Amillennialists see the victory and suffering that believers face in this age as aligning with Revelation's description of the millennium. They also believe that Satan is currently bound and cannot prevent the spread of the gospel in the world, but he can try to harm the Church. Amillennialists would also say that our current age can be captured by the phrase "the already and not yet." Jesus presently reigns, but His kingdom will be fully realized when He comes at the end of this era and reigns eternally in the new heaven and new earth.

POSTMILLENNIALISM

Postmillennialists agree with amillennialists in their belief that the millennium is a period of time that is figurative and not literal. They also agree on the basic sequence of events during the last days of the world: Christ's return, the general resurrection of both the righteous and the wicked, the final judgment, and the beginning of the new heaven and new earth. They also both agree that Satan is currently bound but will be briefly released toward the end of the millennium to cause rebellion against Christ. However, while amillennialists believe that Christians will experience both suffer-

ing and victory before the return of Christ, postmillennialists believe that Christians will increasingly gain influence and experience mostly victory toward the end of the world. In this view, the world will become more and more open to the gospel, and there will be a period of great righteousness and peace before Jesus returns to the earth.

CLASSICAL PREMILLENNIALISM

Christians who hold the classical premillennialism view believe that Jesus will come back after a tribulation period in the world. They believe He will raise all believers to be with Him, and then He will reign over the earth in a millennial kingdom with them for one-thousand years. They see the millennial kingdom as not a figurative period of time but as a literal amount of time that is yet to occur. During Christ's millennial reign, Satan will be bound in a pit, but he will briefly be released at the end of the millennium, causing some people to rebel against Christ. The Lord will end this rebellion, and there will be a resurrection for all of the wicked, who will then face the final judgment. After this judgment, the new heaven and new earth will begin.

DISPENSATIONAL PREMILLENNIALISM

The key difference between classical premillennialism and dispensational premillennialism is the belief that Jesus will rapture believers before a period of tribulation. This tribulation period is known as the "great tribulation," which will be seven years of satanic influence on the earth that will progressively get worse and worse. In this view, Jesus will rapture all who believe in Him before this period of time, and then He will return with His saints after this period ends. Then Christ will set up His millennial kingdom. The events that follow this happen in the same sequence as those described in classical premillennialism.

> *The Lord has graciously revealed to us what is coming at the end of His redemptive story in Scripture.*

Together, we will live happily in God's light and worship Him joyfully for eternity.

What is *the* Gospel?

Thank you for reading and enjoying this study with us! We are abundantly grateful for the Word of God, the instruction we glean from it, and the ever-growing understanding it provides for us of God's character. We are also thankful that Scripture continually points to one thing in innumerable ways: the gospel.

We remember our brokenness when we read about the fall of Adam and Eve in the garden of Eden (Genesis 3), where sin entered into a perfect world and maimed it. We remember the necessity that something innocent must die to pay for our sin when we read about the atoning sacrifices in the Old Testament. We read that we have all sinned and fallen short of the glory of God (Romans 3:23) and that the penalty for our brokenness, the wages of our sin, is death (Romans 6:23). We all need grace and mercy, but most importantly, we all need a Savior.

We consider the goodness of God when we realize that He did not plan to leave us in this dire state. We see His promise to buy us back from the clutches of sin and death in Genesis 3:15. And we see that promise accomplished with Jesus Christ on the cross. Jesus Christ knew no sin yet became sin so that we might become righteous through His sacrifice (2 Corinthians 5:21). Jesus was tempted in every way that we are and lived sinlessly. He was reviled yet still yielded Himself for our sake, that we may have life abundant in Him. Jesus lived the perfect life that we could not live and died the death that we deserved.

The gospel is profound yet simple. There are many mysteries in it that we will never understand this side of heaven, but there is still overwhelming weight to its implications in this life. The gospel tells of our sinfulness and God's goodness and a gracious gift that compels a response. We are saved by grace through faith, which means that we rest with faith in the grace that Jesus Christ displayed on the cross (Ephesians 2:8–9). We cannot save ourselves from our brokenness or do any amount of good works to merit God's favor. Still, we can have faith that what Jesus accomplished in His death, burial, and resurrection was more than enough for our salvation and our eternal delight. When we accept God, we are commanded to die to ourselves and our sinful desires and live a life worthy of the calling we have received (Ephesians 4:1). The gospel compels us to be sanctified, and in so doing, we are conformed to the likeness of Christ Himself. This is hope. This is redemption. This is the gospel.

GENESIS 3:15

I will put hostility between you and the woman, and between your offspring and her offspring. He will strike your head, and you will strike his heel.

ROMANS 3:23

For all have sinned and fall short of the glory of God.

ROMANS 6:23

For the wages of sin is death, but the gift of God is eternal life in Christ Jesus our Lord.

2 CORINTHIANS 5:21

He made the one who did not know sin to be sin for us, so that in him we might become the righteousness of God.

EPHESIANS 2:8-9

For you are saved by grace through faith, and this is not from yourselves; it is God's gift—not from works, so that no one can boast.

EPHESIANS 4:1-3

Therefore I, the prisoner in the Lord, urge you to walk worthy of the calling you have received, with all humility and gentleness, with patience, bearing with one another in love, making every effort to keep the unity of the Spirit through the bond of peace.

BIBLIOGRAPHY

Carson, D. A., ed. *NIV Biblical Theology Study Bible: Follow God's Redemptive Plan as It Unfolds throughout Scripture*. Grand Rapids: Zondervan, 2018.

Chapell, Bryan. *Gospel Transformation Study Bible: Christ in All of Scripture, Grace for All of Life*. Wheaton, IL: Crossway, 2013.

Clark, Andrew, Debra Reid, and Martin Maser, ed. *NIV Bible Speaks Today Study Bible*. Nottingham, UK: InterVarsity Press, 2020.

Constable, Thomas L. "Notes on Revelation." *Sonic Light*. Plano Bible Chapel. 2022. https://www.planobiblechapel.org/tcon/notes/html/nt/revelation/revelation.htm.

Dennis, Lane T., and Wayne Grudem, ed. *The ESV Study Bible*. Wheaton, IL: Crossway, 2008.

Dennis, Lane T., and Wayne Grudem, ed. *The ESV Study Bible*. Wheaton, IL: Crossway Bibles, 2011.

Dennis, Lane T., Wayne Grudem, and J. I. Packer, ed. *The ESV Women's Study Bible*. Wheaton, IL: Crossway, 2020.

Dunn, James D. G. *The Epistles to the Colossians and to Philemon: A Commentary on the Greek Text*. Grand Rapids: Eerdmans, 2014.

Fee, Gordon D., and Douglas K. Stuart. *How to Read the Bible Book by Book: A Guided Tour*. Grand Rapids: Zondervan, 2014.

Geisler, Norman L. *A Popular Survey of the Old Testament*. Grand Rapids: Baker Academic, 1977.

Geisler, Norman L. *A Popular Survey of the New Testament*. Grand Rapids: Baker Academic, 2007.

Gregg, Steve. *Revelation: Four Views, A Parallel Commentary, Revised & Updated Edition*. Nashville: Thomas Nelson Inc, 2013.

Grudem, Wayne A. *1 Peter: An Introduction and Commentary*, vol. 17. Tyndale New Testament Commentaries. Downers Grove, IL: InterVarsity Press, 1988.

Guthrie, Donald. *Hebrews: An Introduction and Commentary*, vol. 15. Tyndale New Testament Commentaries. Downers Grove, IL: InterVarsity Press, 1983.

Keener, Craig S. *The IVP Bible Background Commentary: New Testament*. Downers Grove, IL: IVP Academic, 2014.

Ligonier. "The Son of Man Amid The Lampstands." *Ligonier Ministries*. September 29, 2020. https://www.ligonier.org/learn/devotionals/the-son-of-man-amid-the-lampstands.

Morris, Leon. *Revelation: An Introduction and Commentary*, vol. 20. Tyndale New Testament Commentaries. Downers Grove, IL: InterVarsity Press, 1987.

Sproul, R. C., ed. *The Reformation Study Bible*. Sanford, FL: Reformation Trust Publishing, 2015.

Stott, John R. *The Letters of John: An Introduction and Commentary*, vol. 19. Tyndale New Testament Commentaries. Downers Grove, IL: InterVarsity Press, 1988.

Turner, Alli, and Jennie Heideman, ed. *The Theology Handbook*. Hanover, MD: The Daily Grace Co.®, 2021.

Youngblood, Ronald F., ed. *Nelson's Illustrated Bible Dictionary*. Nashville: Thomas Nelson, 2014.

Thank you for studying
God's Word with us!

CONNECT WITH US
@thedailygraceco
@dailygracepodcast

CONTACT US
info@thedailygraceco.com

SHARE
#thedailygraceco

VISIT US ONLINE
www.thedailygraceco.com

MORE DAILY GRACE
The Daily Grace® App
Daily Grace® Podcast